Understanding Dyslexia and
Other Learning Disabilities

UNDERSTANDING DYSLEXIA AND OTHER LEARNING DISABILITIES

Linda Siegel

Pacific Educational Press
Vancouver, Canada

Copyright © Linda Siegel 2013

ISBN: 978-1-926966-29-8

Published by Pacific Educational Press
Faculty of Education
University of British Columbia
411 – 2389 Health Sciences Mall
Vancouver, BC V6T 1Z3

Telephone: 604-822-5385
Fax: 604-822-6603
Email: pep.admin@ubc.ca
Website: www.pacificedpress.ca

We acknowledge the financial support of the Government of Canada through the
Canada Book Fund (CBF) for our publishing activities.

Library and Archives Canada Cataloguing in Publication
Siegel, Linda, 1942–
        Understanding dyslexia and other learning disabilities
/ Linda Siegel.
Includes bibliographical references and index.
Issued also in electronic format.
ISBN 978-1-926966-29-8
        1. Dyslexia. 2. Learning disabilities. 3. Learning
disabilities—Diagnosis. 4. Learning disabled—Case studies.
I. Title.
LC4708.S53 2013   371.91′44   C2012-905974-9

Cover image: The sculpture *Nomade* by artist Jaume Plensa.
Credit: gianliguori, canstockphoto.com

Design and layout: Sharlene Eugenio
Editing: Barbara Kuhne
Copy editing: Grace Yaginuma
Proofreading: Patricia Wolfe
Indexing: Stephen Ullstrom

Printed in Canada

16 15 14 13   1 2 3 4

For my parents, Paula and Syd Feldman, my children, Laura and Jeffrey, and my grandchildren, Benjamin, Anna, and Sophie.

Contents

Foreword

This book is about learning disabilities and the destruction that they can potentially cause in many lives, but it is also about the opportunity for success that lies within the grasp of individuals with learning disabilities. Siegel's motivation for writing it is summed up in a single sentence: "I want us to understand individuals with learning disabilities as whole people and to see beyond the problems." With this guiding principle, she provides strategies that will be helpful for teachers, parents, and others who wish to provide support to people with dyslexia and other learning disabilities.

Siegel, an internationally known authority in the field of learning disabilities, offers a unique perspective in this volume on what learning disabilities are, what they mean to those who experience them, and how others may view them. She does this by describing many famous, talented individuals who had learning disabilities; highlighting the symptoms, negative impacts, and potential solutions for such varied problems as Pablo Picasso's dyslexia, Agatha Christie's writing disability, and Winston Churchill's math disability; and then pairing several of these with case studies of children she has actually worked with in her own practice. In addition, she introduces the reader to past and current authors whose writings include characters with learning disabilities and modern educators who have written books about their own learning disabilities and the challenges of becoming a teacher. These anecdotes keep the reader engaged, make the volume highly understandable, and drive home not only how people with learning disabilities struggle and what types of problems they face, but also the extraordinary potential they may have.

I strongly endorse Siegel's explanation of why using IQ tests as a diagnostic criterion for learning disabilities is invalid. Siegel's own research, which has been widely published, was seminal in challenging what is known as the achievement–IQ discrepancy definition of learning disabilities. In the 1980s, the basic criterion for identifying a learning disability was discrepancy between a person's IQ score and his or her reading and math scores.

Siegel and other researchers have demonstrated that IQ scores are irrelevant in diagnosing learning disabilities. Unfortunately, however, some people continue to support this outdated notion and, as a consequence, many children have been prevented from receiving the help they need in a timely way (if ever). In this book, Siegel very clearly lays out the results of her research so that parents, teachers, and others, including people who have a learning disability, can understand why IQ testing is not necessary to diagnose a learning disability.

Siegel explains why the process whereby schools require formal assessment of learning disabilities before students receive the help they need creates a barrier for families because of the very high cost of private assessment. She argues in favour of less complex testing, early intervention, and treating all children with respect. While it is true that schools often require diagnostic assessment, some schools are successfully implementing what are called "Response to Intervention" or "Response to Instruction" (RTI) programs. In these situations, all students are screened for difficulties and those who are struggling are closely monitored and given additional instructional attention in small groups or individually. The RTI system therefore allows teachers to provide assistance to struggling students without waiting for diagnostic assessment.

For some students, screening followed by instructional assistance is enough to avert more serious learning problems; for others, it may help to stem the tide of falling behind peers, and for still others, it can demonstrate that full assessment and more intensive intervention are needed. RTI represents an improvement, but it is not enough for those more severely affected with dyslexia or other learning disabilities. It does not fully allay the concern about delays in identifying those with severe learning problems who do not respond to increased intensity of traditional instruction and heightened individual attention. As Siegel notes, "even the best teaching may fail in the case of a dyslexic person," so even with high-quality instruction and a robust intervention program, children with dyslexia and/or other severe learning disabilities will need special instructional approaches, including, in some cases, techniques that circumvent reading to some extent (audio books, audiotaping of lectures, use of other technologies).

Siegel advocates focusing on the strengths of individuals with learning disabilities and finding ways to help either remediate or compensate for their weaknesses. I concur that both social-emotional support and targeted educational or vocational assistance are crucially important: one without the other is not enough. The key to remediation of learning disabilities is to find ways to help students learn, using alternative approaches as necessary, so that they gain the information and skills that will enable them to cope in life, find gainful employment, and feel fulfilled and successful.

Siegel also provides survival tactics for individuals with learning disabilities. Key among them are maintaining a positive outlook and a sense of humour, as well as learning to be one's own best advocate. For parents, she offers tips for advocating for their children in the schools and ways to spot what she calls "snake oil" cures. Siegel warns: "The treatment road is littered with charlatans who promise the world and merely empty the pockets of unsuspecting consumers." Knowing what to look for and what to avoid with regard to treatment options is critical. People who must navigate this often confusing and frustrating path—both individuals with learning disabilities and those seeking to help them—will find this volume engaging, enlightening, and helpful.

— Peggy McCardle, President of Peggy McCardle Consulting, LLC; former Chief of the Child Development and Behavior Branch of the *Eunice Kennedy Shriver* National Institute of Child Health and Human Development.

Introduction
A Wake-Up Call

We live in the midst of an educational tragedy. Schools are failing to identify and treat many children with dyslexia and other learning disabilities.

There is a battle among parents, teachers, educational bureaucrats, and related professionals, with children caught in the crossfire. There are no guns, tanks, and explosives in this conflict. The weapons in this struggle are complicated laws, requirements for extensive testing to identify a learning disability, destruction of students' self-esteem, belittlement of parents' and teachers' concerns, inadequate teacher training, blaming academic failure on behavioural problems, and erecting senseless barriers to reform.

The result is tragic. Many children who struggle with learning become nameless, faceless ghosts haunting our schools and later our jails and mental institutions, or living dangerous and aimless lives as homeless people on our streets. Some die at a young age from drug overdoses or suicide, the ultimate nightmare of parents.

Children are not the only casualties. Adults also suffer from learning disabilities that were not recognized when they were in school and were never treated. Depression, anxiety, and deep feelings of inadequacy often prevent adults with learning disabilities from developing close relationships, finding rewarding employment, and living happy and productive lives.

This book is a journey into the world of learning disabilities from a variety of perspectives. I begin by describing learning disabilities and how we know that a person has a learning disability. Trouble spelling words, slow reading, memory lapses, illegible handwriting, and the inability to calculate the tip in a restaurant or do simple calculations are problems that plague people with learning disabilities. If these difficulties occur frequently, not just occasionally, they are signs of a learning disability. Dyslexia, which is a reading disability, is often misunderstood as a problem with reversing letters or not seeing words properly. In reality, it is a language problem. Difficulties with mathematics are often overlooked, but a mathematics disability, sometimes called dyscalculia, is as common as dyslexia.

The assessment of learning disabilities is often excessively complex and bureaucratic. I present a simple, inexpensive, and effective method to identify children who are at risk for dyslexia and other learning disabilities. But simply identifying learning disabilities is not enough; we must provide assistance to those who have them. Many people, both children and adults, who need help are not receiving it. I explore the reasons for this and propose some solutions. There are many dedicated and caring teachers, but often their hands are tied because they are held hostage by a bureaucratic system that does not put children's needs first. Improving teacher training is an important step. Systematic early identification and intervention for children who are struggling are also key, so that learning difficulties are not compounded by children's frustration, loss of self-esteem, acting out, and being bullied. Recent advances in technology and new methods of providing remedial help for people with learning disabilities are all part of the solution.

Our understanding of learning disabilities developed gradually, (and not without some missteps along the road). Long before physicians and educators identified learning disabilities in the early 1960s, writers Jane Austen and George Eliot described the world of people with learning disabilities. I draw on their insights as well as those of other writers who have provided portraits of people with learning disabilities in literature. I also include true stories of children and adults with learning disabilities. In direct and eloquent language, they tell us the inside story about what the stumbling blocks are and what is helpful. Ignoring what their experiences show us can have dire consequences.

Many people with learning disabilities also have some special talents. Recognizing and nurturing the talents of all children go a long way towards overcoming the obstacles of learning disabilities. Agatha Christie, Winston Churchill, Pablo Picasso, William Butler Yeats, Susan Hampshire, and Greg Louganis all suffered from learning disabilities, yet became very successful. We can learn from their stories how to support children with learning disabilities by focusing on their strengths rather than just their disabilities.

Solving the problem of learning disabilities is within our grasp. But it will take dedication and a desire to succeed. This book aims to provide strategies and ammunition for the battle. I invite you, the reader, to join me on this journey.

PART I

Types of Learning Disabilities

1

The Giant with Dyslexia

Imagine a man four metres (thirteen feet) tall. When he strides down the street, people follow his movements with staring eyes, watching apprehensively as he takes one stride for every three steps of an average person. This man is Rubeus Hagrid, a friendly and compassionate giant who is an important character in the Harry Potter books by J. K. Rowling.[1]

Hagrid is a sympathetic character; readers are drawn to him because he is compassionate and helpful. Hagrid's job is to take care of "strange and monstrous creatures" and "magical animals." The students go to him for tea and sympathy but try to avoid his rock cookies.

However, Hagrid has a problem: he is dyslexic. Hagrid's spelling is terrible. In the beginning of the movie *Harry Potter and the Sorcerer's Stone*, the central character, Harry Potter, receives a birthday cake from Hagrid, who has come to take Harry to Hogwarts School, a school to train young people in the art of magic. The message on the cake is "HAPPEE BIRTHDAE HARRY."[2]

Hagrid's spelling difficulties haunt him. When Harry asks Hagrid the name of the wizard who killed Harry's parents, Hagrid is forced to reveal his spelling problem. He cannot say the name out loud because everyone is afraid that saying the name of this evil wizard will bring him and all his terrible deeds back. Harry suggests that Hagrid write down the name, but Hagrid refuses because he cannot spell it. Dreading the consequences but unable to spell, Hagrid blurts out the forbidden name, Voldemort.

Like many people with dyslexia, Hagrid has terrible handwriting, "an untidy scrawl." When the house-elf, Dobby, tries to hide some letters from Harry, the plot fails because Harry sees one on which the address is written in "a scribble that looked as though it was from the Hogwarts gamekeeper, Hagrid."

Along with spelling and writing problems, Hagrid is sometimes at a loss for words and is not a glib and fluent talker. Many people with dyslexia have language and word-finding difficulties. Hagrid is enthusiastic and kind-hearted, but his slow speech, lack of verbal skills, and short-term memory problems are misinterpreted as stupidity.

Hagrid teaches a class called "The Care of Magical Creatures." When an inspector, Professor Umbridge, comes to Hagrid's class to evaluate his teaching, she uses gestures to accompany her words as if Hagrid does not understand English. Mocking Hagrid, she mimes walking among the students and says that she is going to ask them questions. She points at her mouth to indicate talking as a way of indicating just how stupid Hagrid is. She implies that Hagrid does not speak clearly, and she encourages students to say that they do not understand him.[3]

Bullies are a plague to people with dyslexia; they seize on their weaknesses and torment them. Accounts of the lives of people with dyslexia are riddled with references to the bullying and the teasing that they have received and how inadequate these insults made them feel. Hagrid suffers a similar fate and is the brunt of teasing. The bully, Draco Malfoy, who is Harry's nemesis, makes fun of Hagrid and calls him stupid. When Harry tells him to shut up, Malfoy says, "Maybe he's been messing with stuff that's too *big* for him." Like bullies everywhere, Malfoy encourages his friends, Crabbe and Goyle, to join in mocking Hagrid. They delight in laughing at Hagrid's "stupidity" and tease Harry that Hagrid will be fired. Malfoy even calls Hagrid a "moron."

Hagrid is also the victim of racism. He is half giant, half wizard, not the pure-blooded wizard ideal. The evil temporary head of Hogwarts calls Hagrid a "great half-breed oaf."

Is Hagrid Dyslexic?

Yes, I believe the evidence suggests that he is, but only J. K. Rowling knows for sure. Hagrid is a fictional character, but Rowling's portrayal of him mirrors the reality of the life of a dyslexic. Hagrid has spelling problems, very poor handwriting, difficulties finding the right words, and memory problems. These signs mark him as dyslexic.

But Hagrid is not just a dyslexic. He is also a kind and caring person who is not afraid to shed a tear for a person or animal that has died or been seriously injured. And he is loyal to his friends, bravely defending them.

The character Hagrid illustrates that people with dyslexia, like all of us, are complicated, multi-dimensional people who defy mere labels. In this book I explore the abilities, as well as the problems, of people with dyslexia and other learning disabilities. I want us to understand individuals with learning disabilities as whole people and to see beyond the problems.

The next chapters introduce real people with dyslexia and other learning disabilities.

2

Spelling Test Terror

"I'm sick. I can't eat." Nine-year-old Rob sat at the kitchen table stirring his Dyno-Bites cereal soaked in milk, lifting spoonfuls and watching the cereal fall off the spoon.[1] He looked out the window. It was the kind of Friday morning in November that everyone except the sidewalk umbrella-sellers hated—cold, drizzly, windy, and with grey skies and no sign of the sun. Rob stared at the cereal floating in the milk; he pushed the bits around and made little mushy piles.

Rob's mother looked anxiously at him and said, "Rob, eat your cereal. You need to leave in five minutes. It's eight fifteen. You'll miss the bus."

"I can't go to school. I'm too sick," he mumbled. "I think I have a fever. My stomach hurts. My head feels funny."

His mother touched his forehead. "You don't feel warm," she said, puzzled. "I don't think you have a fever."

"I feel hot."

"I'm sure you'll feel better in a few minutes."

"No I won't. It really hurts."

"Go brush your teeth and get your books and jacket."

Leaving his favourite cereal uneaten, Rob pushed the chair away from the table and, clutching his stomach, walked slowly into his room and fell onto the bed.

His mother appeared at the doorway. "Okay, I guess that I'll have to take your temperature."

"Okay," Rob groaned.

Rob lay on his bed staring at the hockey poster on his wall and thought, "I don't want to go to school."

His mother stuck a thermometer in his mouth before leaving the room. He grabbed the thermometer and put it near the baseboard heater. He hoped the thermometer would heat up because he really hated school, and having a fever would make his mother keep him at home.

Friday was spelling test day. He really hated spelling tests. Those little words were the worst: *when, which, been.* The longer ones weren't much better either. He hoped the thermometer trick would work. Of course, he had to be careful. He would be in big trouble if he broke the thermometer because it got too hot.

He prayed to God, but praying was supposed to be for important things like when your grandmother was sick and you prayed for her to be better. You were not supposed to pray about a spelling test.

Rob thought to himself, "If only I could miss today, then I would have the weekend." His hockey practice was the next day, but if he were sick his mother would not let him go. She might make him stay in bed. He would make sure he was better by tomorrow. He hated to miss hockey. Which did he hate more— missing hockey practice or taking a spelling test? This was a really hard question. He heard his mother's footsteps and stuck the thermometer back in his mouth.

His mother appeared in the doorway and came over to his bed. "No fever," she said as she looked at the thermometer.

"My stomach hurts," he whined.

"Come on, I'll drive you to school. You missed the bus." Rob grabbed his lunch bag with his cheese sandwich, a banana, and a brownie, and ran to the car.

Rob's attempted trick with the thermometer had not worked. He had to face the horror of the spelling test. He hoped that aliens would land their spaceship in the schoolyard and kidnap him. On second thought, that might not be too much fun if they were mean aliens and he might miss hockey practice and his parents. Maybe the school would burn down before he got there. That would not be too good because people might get hurt. Maybe Ms. Johnson would be absent and they would have a substitute teacher. They could tell the substitute that there was no spelling test. But Tiffany and Jason, who always got 100 per cent on the spelling test—even with words like *possession*, *character*, and *opportunity*—would tell that there really was supposed to be a spelling test.

"Here we are, Rob. Good luck on the spelling test," his mother called as he slowly got out of the car. He shuffled towards the school. Maybe an earthquake would occur far enough away so that no one was hurt, but close enough to rattle the windows and have the spelling test cancelled. Unfortunately, that was unlikely.

Then he had an inspiration: an earthquake drill! That would save him. He liked earthquake and fire drills; students missed about forty-five minutes of class whenever there was such a drill.

He looked at the clock—forty-five minutes to the spelling test. He prayed for an earthquake drill. Now he was getting hungry. He should have eaten the cereal. They were doing arithmetic work-sheets, multiplication of two- and three-digit numbers. It was not so bad. At least he could do math. Thirty minutes to go. He prayed again for an earthquake drill, even though he knew that people were not supposed to waste their prayers on earthquake drills. He looked at the clock again. Only five minutes till the spelling test. The earthquake drill had better come soon.

What Is Dyslexia?

Why did the prospect of a spelling test cause Rob to feel so terrified and anxious? The answer is simple—he has a learning disability called dyslexia. Having dyslexia means that Rob struggles with reading. Compared to other children of his age, it is much more difficult for him to pronounce and understand the words on a page.[2] Even when he is able to read the words correctly, he reads quite slowly. Individuals with dyslexia struggle to figure out the sounds of the letters. The ability to sound out the letters in a word is called a *phonological* skill, which means knowing the pronunciation of letters.

In order to understand how people read and why some struggle with reading, you can take a simple reading test. Below are two lists of words. Read each word out loud if you are alone or silently if there are other people in the room.

List 1	List 2
the	anacampserote
and	ucalegon
sit	mithridatism
when	qualtagh
book	groak

If you are like most people, list 1 was easy to read: you just looked at the words and you knew how to pronounce them. It was an automatic process. For list 2, if you are like most people, you broke each word down into syllables or letters and sounded out each part and then used memory skills to put them together. These are real English words, but very obscure ones; because you have likely never seen them before, you used a different technique to read them. Even if you saw those words in a sentence and could guess the meaning, you still would need your phonological skills to pronounce them.

Rob had difficulty in reading words, particularly in knowing the sounds of the letters—the skills required for reading the words in list 2. Problems with knowing the sounds of letters and letter combinations are at the heart of dyslexia, not just in English but in any language. This ability is sometimes called word attack or phonological processing. Children with dyslexia struggle with decoding when they are learning to read and take much more time to learn this skill than children without dyslexia. Even when they have learned decoding, they are slower readers than others of the same age and have much more trouble with words of two or more syllables. Children with dyslexia struggle so hard with phonological processing that they sometimes forget the beginning of the word by the time they get to the end, and have to start over. Or in attacking a long word, they may forget the beginning of the sentence.

Here are some examples of errors that Rob made when I asked him to read a list of words:

Word on the list	What he read
finger	fire
felt	fat
light	laugh
which	watch
together	things

Most nine-year-olds without dyslexia would read these words correctly. These errors provide clues about how Rob is reading. He obviously had trouble sounding out words, and his answers did not match the printed words exactly. He said the sound of the first letter correctly, but it seemed as if he just looked at the first letter and guessed the rest of the word. For example, in attempting to read *together*, he guessed *things*. Sometimes Rob seemed to recognize some of the other letters in the words, but this was not always the case. For example, the *i* in *finger* and *fire* has a different sound; one is a long vowel and one is a short vowel. When reading *felt*, he omitted the sound of the letter *l* and used the wrong vowel. People with dyslexia sometimes omit letters because they may not hear all the sounds in a word. Even the *gh* was a problem; it is silent in *light* but pronounced as *f* in *laugh*. Three of the letters match in *which* and *watch*, but the middle of the two words are quite different. Rob seemed to remember what words look like but had trouble sounding them out. Many people with dyslexia have trouble with vowels in English because these vowels have many different sounds—nineteen in total.

One of the ways to test for sounding-out ability is to have people read out loud what are called *pseudowords*—that is, pronounceable combinations of letters that are not real words in the language being tested. You can read such pseudowords only by sounding out the letters—for example, *hap, fim, mell, loast, qualidation,* and *bafmotbem.* You may wonder, why read something that is not a word? If you ask people to read real words, they may have seen the words before and guess the pronunciation from memory. When people encounter a new word such as *tetrachloroethylene* or *organometallic,* they need to break it down into smaller pieces and sound them out. Reading of pseudowords is the best way to test phonological or sounding-out skills. Rob could read some of the simple words, such as *hap*, *fim*, and *mel*, but below are some of the errors that he made on a pseudoword reading test:

Pseudowords on the page	What he read
pawk	paw
floxy	fox
chur	chair
loast	last
pog	pig

These are pseudowords that most children his age who are not dyslexic would be able to read easily. Note that although Rob was told that these were not real words, he turned the pseudowords into words. He had problems with many of the sounds in these pseudowords. He usually read the first letter correctly but had difficulty with most of the vowels and some of the consonants. He read *loast* as *last* because of his difficulty with vowels. A younger child without dyslexia might read *loast* as *lo-ast* (a two-syllable pseudoword with two vowels). The usual response of non-dyslexic readers if they cannot read a pseudoword is to sound it out, close in pronunciation to the word they see in front of them, but the pronunciation is not perfect. Compared to others of the same age, people who are not dyslexic usually have no trouble with pseudoword tests, while those with dyslexia really struggle with them.

Along with reading, spelling is also a problem for people with dyslexia. If we look at Rob's spelling, we can understand why he was terrified of spelling tests. Here are some examples of his spelling errors:

Word that was dictated	What he wrote
cook	kuk
make	mak
reach	rech

Most children his age could spell these words correctly. Rob had difficulty with all the vowels. Like many children with dyslexia, he also wrote slowly and his handwriting was difficult to read. Many people with dyslexia also have trouble remembering what they read. Remembering telephone numbers, PIN codes, zip and postal codes, and multiplication tables can all be difficult for people with dyslexia.

The percentage of people with dyslexia varies depending on how it is defined, but it is reasonable to say that between 4 and 10 per cent of the population have significant reading problems. A similar number of people have a mathematics disability, and some people have difficulties with both reading and mathematics.[3] We know that dyslexia is a neurological disorder that has a genetic basis. It is *not* caused by parents failing to read to a child or by poor eyesight, inability to pay attention, a parents' divorce, or emotional turmoil in the family.

English Bashing

English is the most irregular alphabetic language in the world. Consider the words *have, says, said, does, should, through,* and *rough.* You cannot pronounce them by using the letter sounds of English. Languages such as Spanish, Italian, and German are quite regular; that is, you can pronounce words just by knowing the sounds of the letters. Does the irregular nature of the English language result in more dyslexics or more difficulty for dyslexics? The answer is no. Dyslexia is found in all languages, and dyslexics have the same phonological problems in all languages. In a language like Mandarin, visual memory is also important. Chinese dyslexics may have visual memory difficulties in addition to phonological problems.

Much to the surprise of nearly everyone, I argue that English is a good language for people with dyslexia. Learning to read in English encourages you to use two reading strategies: sounding out for words like *cat, stop, mice, like, hit* and visual memory for words like *have, said, through, could*. More predictable languages do not encourage visual memory for words because simply decoding the letters works quite well. I watched a nine-year-old Italian dyslexic girl struggle with reading. She tried to pronounce each letter, but remembering the sounds of the letters was difficult for her. If she were reading English, she would not be so tempted to read letter by letter because she would have learned a second reading strategy.

Myths about Dyslexia

Sometimes people think that having dyslexia means that a person sees and writes letters and words backwards (for example, the word *was* read as *saw* or *b* and *d* are confused). This popular myth is not true. Some people with dyslexia have this problem, but most do not. Young children who are just learning to read and write may reverse letters and words, but it does not mean that they have dyslexia. These reversal errors occur as a normal part of learning to read.

Dyslexia is a language problem and means that a person sometimes lacks the abilities to remember the sounds of the letters, read long words, remember what he or she has read, and find the right words or remember what something is called. Some people with dyslexia have trouble finding the word that they want to say;

when they cannot remember the name of something, they may describe it instead. For example, instead of saying "carrot," they might say "the long and orange thing that grows in the ground." Some people with dyslexia have more subtle difficulties with language and may make mistakes in verb tenses and/or vocabulary. I have even heard of several people with dyslexia who, frustrated by their language problems, made up their own languages, understandable only to them.

Another popular myth is that boys (and men) are much more likely to be dyslexic than girls (and women). The actual ratio is about the same; neither gender has a monopoly on dyslexia. Earlier reports of many more males with dyslexia arose because boys who exhibited difficult behaviour at school were more likely to be referred for testing.[4] Girls who had reading and/or mathematics problems typically sat quietly in a corner and did not misbehave, so they were not identified as having problems. When the reading levels of large samples of children are tested— for example, all the children from one school district—there are slightly more males than females with reading problems but the difference is not significant.[5]

The "Dyslexic Einstein" Myth

If you asked people on the street to name the most brilliant person in the world, they would probably say Albert Einstein. This "father of modern physics," who invented the general theory of relativity and won a Nobel Prize in 1921 for his discoveries, is the ultimate symbol of intelligence. His name is a household word that denotes brilliance.

The idea has been perpetuated that Einstein was dyslexic.[6] Sometimes it is also said that he failed mathematics in school. Neither of these statements is true. Quite to the contrary,

Einstein was an excellent student in nearly all school subjects, was at the head of his class, and typically brought home a brilliant report card.

The evidence of Einstein's academic achievements is overwhelming. From an early age, mathematics fascinated him. His uncle Jakob introduced him to algebra by explaining it was a game of hunting for the "animal x" in equations.[7] The same uncle introduced him to geometry at the age of twelve. Einstein relished the beauty and elegance of this branch of mathematics and derived satisfaction from doing the proofs. He obtained a geometry textbook in advance and solved all the problems before the geometry class began. By age twelve, he devoured popular science books introduced to him by a medical student who was a frequent guest in the Einstein household. As a young boy, Einstein read Kant with apparent ease and understanding. It is very unlikely that a dyslexic young person could do so.

In grade 10 at the Luitpold Gymnasium (the equivalent of secondary school) in Munich, Germany, Einstein was near the top of his class and excelled in Latin, Greek, German, mathematics, and physics. He barely passed French but enjoyed the logic of Latin, displaying the analytic skills that later helped him make his discoveries.

There is no evidence of poor spelling or incorrect grammar in Einstein's letters. If he had been dyslexic, we would certainly see spelling and grammatical errors in his writing. As a young man working in a patent office, he edited poorly written and ungrammatical applications. A person with dyslexia could not have done this type of editorial work.

From early childhood, Einstein was interested in mechanical toys. At the age of two, when he was introduced to his newborn baby sister and told she could be a new toy for him, he responded,

"Yes, but where are its wheels?" His parents hired a tutor for him before he began school, but not for remedial tutoring; this tutoring was designed to enable him to begin school at a younger-than-usual age.

Einstein loved learning and solving puzzles and mathematical problems. He had superior visual-spatial skills and liked to build complex structures using blocks. He was a bit of a daydreamer in school, but is there a student anywhere in the world who has not occasionally succumbed to wandering thoughts unrelated to the material that is being taught in class? He was not a social butterfly; he often preferred to be alone rather than play with other children. However, he was very close to his family and developed strong friendships and romantic relationships throughout his life.

Einstein hated doing the rote memory exercises that were typically required in schools of that time. He disliked the formality of the classroom and having to stand to address the teacher. On the other hand, when he attended a school where he could discuss ideas and interact with the teacher, he showed more enthusiasm. Obviously, he preferred thinking and reasoning over memorization.

As an adult, when he was asked his opinions about school, Einstein commented that the teachers were like sergeants and lieutenants; he likened their behaviour to brutal and sadistic military men who enforced discipline and order. In spite of this, he was a good student.

The idea of Einstein's dyslexia is an urban legend. Perhaps the myth started because he was slow in learning to speak. Early language delay is sometimes seen in children who later become dyslexic. However, early language difficulties are not dyslexia. Even as an adult, Einstein talked slowly and sometimes took a long time to respond. He often repeated sentences to himself before saying them, but this language behaviour is the sign of a careful thinker, not of a dyslexic.

It is easy to see how the myth that Einstein was dyslexic could have been perpetuated. If you were dyslexic or the parent of a dyslexic, it would be immensely gratifying to believe that Einstein was also dyslexic. He was an icon of brilliant intelligence. If you lacked self-esteem or worried about your intelligence, as many people with dyslexia do, identifying with Einstein might be appealing. The "dyslexic Einstein" became a legend to cherish, but it is inappropriate to make him a symbol of dyslexia.

3

Picasso, the Artist with Dyslexia

The paintings of Pablo Picasso (1881–1973) are evocative, innovative, and deceptively simple. Full of bold lines and colours, they remain as vivid images in our memory. As creative as Pablo Picasso was with a brush, his talents did not extend to his schoolwork. Picasso had all the signs of dyslexia, according to the accounts of his friend Jaime Sabartés.[1] Of course, Sabartés did not identify it as dyslexia; he merely described what sound like the symptoms that we associate with dyslexia. For example, Picasso claimed that he could not learn to read or write before the age of ten and that he could never recall the correct order of the letters of the alphabet. He had trouble learning words and numbers, even though he tried really hard. He also had terrible handwriting, and teachers forced him to write journals in a futile attempt to improve it. The journals were filled with pictures instead of writing. At the age of twelve Picasso could not spell *azul*, the Spanish word for "blue." He said *azul* correctly, but he spelled it *asul*. People with dyslexia frequently make this error; they spell the word the way it sounds, but often this is the incorrect spelling.

Yet he drew pictures all over his school books. At home he drew and painted instead of completing his lessons. He told his granddaughter Marina, "There's no point in being good at school. It serves no purpose. . . . I was hopeless in all subjects. That didn't prevent me from succeeding."[2]

Picasso had to be dragged to school. He hated school, only surviving it because he was allowed to paint and draw. He would stare at the clock, as if he could will the endless hours to pass. As Picasso told his friend, because he was a "bad" student, the teacher banished him from the classroom to a small bare room with just a bench to sit on. He claimed that he misbehaved on purpose so he could escape the classroom and draw to his heart's content without anyone bothering him.[3]

Picasso used every trick to avoid school. He had to be bribed to go to school with the promise of paintbrushes at home. According to biographer John Richardson, Picasso boasted that the young Pablo would throw tantrums and complain that he was ill to try and avoid school.

Picasso would do anything to escape studying. He would wander off to the kitchen and watch the headmaster's wife tend the fire or peel potatoes—anything rather than sit at his desk. The family called in a private tutor, but this did not solve the problem. The young Picasso would rush to the window during his lessons and try to gesture to someone to come and rescue him. School was a nightmare. Picasso said that he tried to concentrate, but schoolwork never sank in. He gave up on school and left at age sixteen.

His biographer Richardson disputes this claim about Picasso's school difficulties. He claims that Picasso was so gifted that it does not make sense that he could not learn to read and write easily. Here Richardson displays his ignorance of learning disabilities. He assumes that Picasso's genius in painting and drawing means that Picasso could not have had a learning disability that caused him to struggle in any areas. A person can be talented in one area but struggle to learn reading or spelling or mathematics. Picasso's extraordinary talent may have been a result, at least partially, of his dyslexia. Some people with dyslexia have extraordinary visual-spatial skills. Even a casual observer of Picasso's work cannot help but see the three-dimensional images, the use of space, and the multiple perspectives in his work.

Why would Picasso invent reading difficulties? Richardson suggests that Picasso might have done so to make his artistic work seem more like that of a genius. I think it is highly unlikely that Picasso invented his difficulty with reading and writing, especially as others in his family corroborated his accounts.

Special Talents

The controversy about whether Picasso could have reading difficulties while being a great artist highlights one of the difficulties many people with dyslexia face. Many people with dyslexia are talented in some areas, leading people to think they could not possibly have problems with reading. In fact, we often fail to appreciate how variable a person's abilities can be. Winston Churchill is a good illustration of this sometimes frustrating combination of real problems and superb skills. He was a brilliant speaker and writer whose precise and colourful use of the English language lives on in our contemporary language. However, he had a mathematics learning disability, which I will discuss in chapter 5.

Many people who have a learning disability also have one or more special talents, such as musical or artistic aptitudes, mechanical abilities, skill at sports, or the ability to dance well. Rob, whose story was introduced in chapter 2, loves to play the piano. To the delight of his piano teacher, he even likes to practise, and he is doing very well. Like many people with dyslexia, Rob struggles to read music but has a good ear and a remarkable memory for music, so he need not rely on reading musical scores. Many dyslexics with musical abilities choose to play guitar or drums because reading music is not as necessary with these instruments. There have been many accomplished musicians who could not read music, including Dave Brubeck, Buddy Rich, John Lennon, and Paul McCartney.

It is important to identify the special talents of people with learning disabilities to help increase their self-esteem and to enable them to reach their full potential.

4

The Case of Agatha Christie: Dysgraphia

I myself was always recognized, though quite kindly,
as the "slow one" of the family.

—Agatha Christie

Agatha Christie (1890–1976) is one of the most famous writers who has ever lived. Her books have sold almost as many copies as the Bible and have been translated into more than a hundred languages. She is known all over the world; her name is a household word in many countries. And yet, in spite of her great success, she believed that she was the slow one in her family.

Christie believed that she was inarticulate and could not keep up with schoolwork. Why did she feel this way? Why did such a successful woman have feelings of inferiority and inadequacy? Christie's story helps us understand the emotional world of people with learning disabilities. It would be easy to blame cold, insensitive parents for feelings of inferiority, but Christie came from a caring family that loved and appreciated her. It would be easy to blame society for not recognizing her talents, but this is obviously also untrue. Christie enjoyed acclaim and prosperity in her lifetime and died a very rich woman. So we cannot blame her family or society, but we also cannot agree with Christie's self-perception. How do we explain the paradox of this rich, famous, and successful woman who felt inferior to others?

Symptoms of a Learning Disability

The answer is simple: Agatha Christie had a learning disability. It may seem paradoxical that a woman who was one of the most popular and prolific writers in the English language had a learning problem. Agatha Christie had the learning disability variously known as "developmental output failure," "written-output disability," "dyscalculia," "dysgraphia," and/or "writing backwardness."

She had all the classic symptoms of a learning disability, but it was not dyslexia. Developmental output failure is a learning disability that is less well known and less well understood than dyslexia. At the time when Agatha Christie was growing up, very little was known about learning disabilities, and the young Agatha suffered a great deal because of her failures to learn. She was a poor speller, she had terrible handwriting, she made many mistakes in arithmetic, and she had trouble learning foreign languages.

Agatha Christie had no difficulty with reading. In fact, just the opposite was the case. She learned to read early and well, in spite of her mother's belief that "no child ought to be allowed to read until it was eight years old."[1] Her family encouraged her to read by giving her books and sending her letters.

Spelling and Writing

In spite of her success with reading, Agatha Christie was a terrible speller. Her spelling was typical of "people who remember words by ear rather than by eye," notes Janet Morgan, one of her biographers.[2] In her autobiography, Christie characterized herself as "an extraordinarily bad speller," not just as a child but even when she was an adult.[3]

Both the spelling and mechanical aspects of writing were a problem for Agatha Christie. Describing her notes to a governess who had retired and whom she missed, Christie says that the notes were badly written, with many spelling mistakes. Her spelling was such a problem that later it forced her to change the title of at least two of her books. She was writing a mystery set in the Caribbean but removed *Caribbean* from the title, changing it to *Nimrud and Its Remains* because she struggled to remember the spelling of *Caribbean*.

Spelling was a chronic problem for Agatha Christie, a problem that persisted throughout her life. Biographer Morgan writes that Christie could not remember how to spell *Frankfurt*. The actual act of writing made her "cross" because she found it difficult. Her older sister, Madge, attempted to help her with spelling and writing, but both Madge and Agatha became very frustrated.

Handwriting and Composition

Agatha Christie writes in her autobiography that the physical act of writing was not nearly as much fun as reading. She makes an interesting comment on the English language, noting that she paid attention to the look of words, not just the letters in the words. In reading English, we all read many words by the "look" because many words cannot be read by sounding them out. Words such as *have, pint, give,* and *giraffe* are irregular and cannot be pronounced using clear rules of pronunciation of the English language. If English followed the rules, *have* should be pronounced with a long *a* to rhyme with *wave* and *save, pint* should be pronounced to rhyme with *mint, give* should be pronounced to rhyme with *five,* and *says* would be pronounced to rhyme with *days.*

Arithmetic

One aspect of developmental output failure is difficulty with computational arithmetic; this is why it is sometimes known as arithmetic and written-output disability or mathematics disability. Agatha Christie's mathematical problem-solving abilities were quite good, but computation was a struggle. Biographer Jeffrey Feinman notes that Agatha Christie had difficulty balancing her bank accounts.[4] Fortunately, she was rich enough to be able to afford accountants to balance her chequebook for her, a luxury that most people with math disabilities do not have.

Agatha Christie did have trouble doing arithmetic under pressure. In her autobiography she says that she sometimes panicked when faced with a mathematics exam and was unable to think and come up with the answers. This type of math phobia and panic when confronted with math problems is quite common in people with this disability.

Learning a Foreign Language

Agatha Christie's difficulty with the mechanics of writing, spelling, and the rote aspects of language extended to French. The disability was quite pronounced and quite surprising, given that as a child she lived for a while in France, had a French governess, and spoke excellent French with the accent of a native speaker. In her autobiography, she wrote that she struggled with French, failing the written tests because she made many spelling mistakes. Her troubles with French were similar to her difficulties with English spelling. Her teachers, obviously unaware of learning disabilities, were perplexed by Agatha's mistakes because she spoke excellent French, had a good grasp of the language, and understood French literature very well. Her spelling difficulties frustrated her and her teachers because she had such good oral language skills. In this regard, nothing much has changed in more than a century; teachers and parents still despair at spelling mistakes. Some of us can spell very well and we lose patience with those who cannot. But those with spelling difficulties really cannot help it. They are trying as hard as they can. Agatha Christie feigned indifference to her difficulties learning how to write French and claimed that she really did not care about her poor spelling. This kind of denial is quite common in individuals with a learning disability because in their hearts they feel that they are stupid and lazy.

Consequences

We now recommend that individuals with this disability learn to type and use a computer to help them compensate for problems with handwriting. According to biographer Derrick Murdoch, Agatha Christie used two fingers on each hand to type, and she claimed, jokingly, that she could write much more quickly than writers who used only one finger of each hand.[5]

Using an audio recorder is another approach that is recommended for this learning disability. By doing so, the mechanics of putting words down on paper do not interfere with the person's imagination and creativity. When Agatha Christie broke her wrist in 1952 and could not write, she turned to a dictating machine, at which she became very successful. According to Morgan, using a dictating machine seemed to help Agatha Christie write more natural-sounding dialogue.

She was clearly interested and competent at solving puzzles in all forms. Morgan notes that she was interested in riddles, bridge, chess, and crosswords, and even in theoretical studies in physics and chemistry.

In summary, the evidence that Agatha Christie had a writing and mathematics learning disability (i.e., developmental output failure) as opposed to a reading disability are as follows: average or above-average intelligence, as shown by her problem-solving skills and the intricate and clear plots in her novels; poor spelling; poor computational arithmetic skills; poor handwriting; difficulty with the written aspects of a foreign language; and good oral language and skills.

Perhaps the story of Agatha Christie will serve as inspiration to people who have struggled with learning disabilities. Agatha Christie's learning disability made her feel stupid, and she was unhappy throughout her life because of it. Unfortunately, her experience is typical of people with learning disabilities; they are often in emotional pain and torment because of the learning difficulties they face.

It is interesting to note that Agatha Christie expressed similar self-doubts and anxiety as William Butler Yeats, as you will see in chapter 7, although they had different kinds of learning disabilities. Individuals who suffer or have suffered from the trauma of a learning disability—and teachers of these students—can gain valuable lessons about tolerance, perseverance, patience, and hope from the early years of struggle with reading, spelling, writing, and arithmetic experienced by Agatha Christie and William Butler Yeats.

What saved Agatha Christie was her persistence; in spite of her spelling and writing difficulties, she kept on with her craft. Her first attempts at writing for publication were not successful, but determination fuelled her successful writing career. Persistence is common in successful people with learning disabilities and is one quality that is responsible for their success. Motivation matters in writing, acting, sports, and any other human endeavour. But it is not enough. Circumstances, a supportive environment, and/or a good mentor can make the difference between success and failure.

Parents of children with learning disabilities often tell me that they are worried about their child's future. I tell them the story of Agatha Christie to give them hope. Of course, not everyone with spelling and writing problems is a talented Agatha Christie, but we should be able to see writing talent beyond poor spelling and handwriting.

A Spelling/Writing Disability

Some people who struggle with writing and spelling, like Agatha Christie, are good readers. I tested Jenny when she was eight years old and in grade 3. She was a good reader; she read words correctly and quickly and understood what she read. However, Jenny had trouble spelling and writing. Below are some samples of her work.

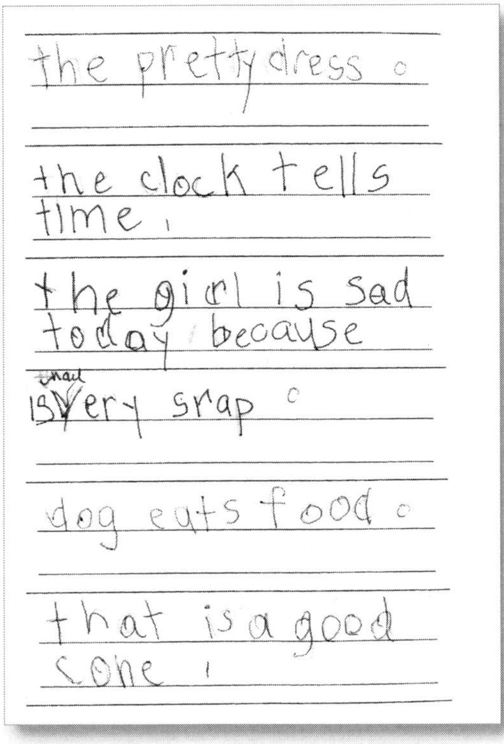

Figure 1. Samples of Jenny's fluency test.

Her handwriting was slow and awkward. I asked her to write some sentences about pictures, and she was supposed to use the three words that I gave her about each picture. The test that I gave her, called the Writing Fluency subtest from the *Woodcock-Johnson III Tests of Achievement*, required her to write as many sentences as she could in a short time.[6] As you can see, she was unable to write complete sentences. Although she described the pictures quite well, she wrote only one complete sentence. She struggled to write the letters, and some are poorly written; the slant is to the left, not to the right, the letters are all different sizes, and sometimes she cannot write on the line. Look at the way that she tries to make the letters *o, g, a, d,* and *v.* You can see the extra lines as she attempts these. Her brain uses so much energy and concentration to try to make the letters that she seems to forget what she is doing. She omits capital letters and periods. She sometimes leaves out *the.* Yet she has the right ideas; putting them down on paper is the problem.

Contrast Jenny's writing with that of Shelley, another eight-year-old in grade 3, reading at the same level. Her letters are neatly formed and fairly even. She uses capitals and periods. She uses *this* instead of *the,* which is more specific.

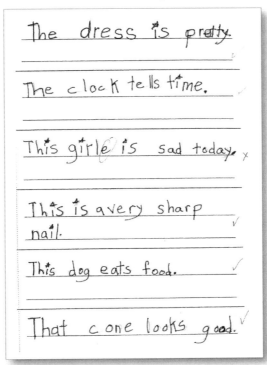

Figure 2. Samples of Shelley's fluency test.

For the next exercise, I asked both girls to write some sentences about pictures without giving them words that they had to use. They just had to look at each picture and write a sentence. These questions were from the Writing Samples subtest of *Woodcock-Johnson III Tests of Achievement.*[7]

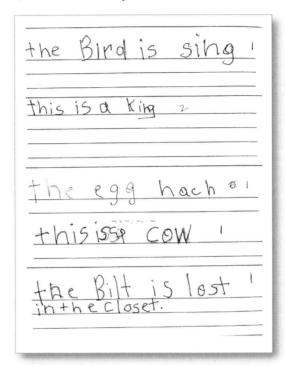

Figure 3. Samples of Jenny's writing test.

The girls could take as much time as they needed. Jenny had trouble completing the sentences; she omitted capitals and periods but sometimes put extra capitals in the middle of the sentence (*Bird* and *Bilt*; the latter was supposed to be *belt*). Her sentences contained some spelling mistakes.

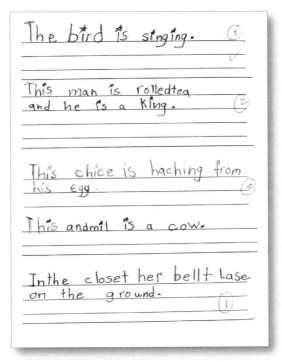

Figure 4. Samples of Shelley's writing test.

Contrast Jenny's writing with Shelley's. Shelley was able to write complete sentences with capitals and periods, and with a neat handwriting. She was able to make her letters easily without extra marks. Her spelling is not perfect; she tries to use some big words. Her spelling is somewhat phonetic—in other words, you can figure out the misspelled word by sounding it out. For example, *rolledtea* means *royalty*, *haching* means *hatching*, and *lase* means *lays*. These errors are typical of children of her age and grade; unlike Jenny, Shelley does not have a writing disability.

A writing/spelling disability such as Jenny's is often overlooked in schools. Teachers and parents assume that children who make the kinds of errors Jenny made are just lazy. I watched Jenny struggle; she was really trying hard. Jenny told me that she hated writing but liked reading. Shelley, on the other hand, wrote effortlessly, confidently, and with enjoyment. Jenny was working so hard to form the letters that she seemed to forget what she wanted to say. Thinking, writing, and remembering at the same time was difficult for her. Her working memory failed her.

These problems often go unrecognized. Having children say what they want to write can help them. Letting them talk into a recording device can show us what they are thinking. Teachers should be careful about marking too many corrections in red ink. I know one adult who has a writing/spelling problem who is now a teacher herself, who refuses to correct the papers of her students in red ink because of her aversion to corrections marked in red. Green, blue, purple, or any other colour is okay. But not red.

Will Jenny's handwriting improve? In my experience, not much. In this case, finding alternative methods, such as typing, is the best solution.

5

Winston Churchill
Famous Orator, Superb Military Strategist, Failure at Mathematics

A quadratic equation belonged to the world of
Alice in Wonderland and the Differential Calculus
was a dragon.

—Winston Churchill on mathematics

Winston Churchill's description of mathematics echoes the feelings of many people with a mathematics disability. For them, the world of numbers, equations, and mathematic problems is populated by evil creatures, designed to make their life miserable. Although we hear much more about dyslexia, it is not the only learning disability. Mathematics disability, sometimes called dyscalculia, is quite common but often goes unrecognized.

Winston Churchill (1874–1965) was a world-renowned politician and an inspiring orator, with a masterful command of the English language. His skill at military strategy enabled him to be one of the powerful players that engineered the Allied victory in World War II. Yet, school was a challenge that almost defeated him.

Churchill despised mathematics, Greek, Latin, and French with an intense hatred later reserved for his wartime enemies. What explains his dismal performance in school? What fuelled his passionate hatred of school subjects? Why did he fail his examinations? Through his autobiography, we learn how he coped with his learning problems and how they also had a profound effect on his self-esteem.

A Mathematics Learning Disability

Winston Churchill did not have dyslexia. However, he did have a mathematics learning disability and also struggled with learning foreign languages. He had chronic difficulties at school, failed examinations, and had private tutors during the summer holidays because he struggled so hard with his studies. According to his report card, his composition was very "feeble" and his spelling was "hopeless." His teachers also noted that he did not know the meaning of hard work. In other words, he was "lazy." Teachers and parents who do not understand learning disabilities think children who make many errors or fail to learn something are lazy. This misconception permeates the attitudes of many adults who encounter children who have trouble learning in school. It is an unfortunate view and further erodes the self-esteem of children with learning disabilities.

Reading and Arithmetic with Tears

As a child, the young Winnie, as he was called, hated learning reading and mathematics. He complained bitterly that reading and mathematics activities took him away from playing with his beloved toy soldiers and his steam engine or just running in the garden. His nurse, Mrs. Everest, attempted to teach him to read. It was horrible drudgery for Winnie. The book that his nurse used was *Reading without Tears*, but Winnie cried tears of frustration. Then, a governess was hired to teach him, but even before he met her, he ran away to the woods to escape her evil clutches. However, he soon made progress in learning letters and words, and throughout his life liked reading and writing. He was not dyslexic.

However, numbers were especially frustrating. He wrote that letters made words and eventually made sense but numbers were the problem. He complained that with numbers, the answers had to be exact and left no room for imagination. Letters and words became easy for him to interpret, but numbers were a different story because problems had to have the exact answer, which often eluded him.

Winston Churchill understood the essence of the difference between reading and mathematics. When you read, the words are in front of you, and if you can decode them, you know their meaning. Solving mathematical equations is different. You need to produce the answer; it is not in front of you.

His dislike for mathematics never abated, becoming worse on his reluctant journey through school.

School Performance

Unlike his later career as a statesman, Churchill's school years were, at best, undistinguished. In fact, they could be more properly described as a dismal failure. The first school that he attended was a boarding school called St. James's School. At this school, flogging with a birch rod for even the most minor infraction was the norm. The young Winnie was frequently at the wrong end of the rod. He made very little progress in his lessons and did not do well in sports. He desperately wanted to go home. His first school report was very poor; he came out at the bottom of the class. That pattern continued throughout school; he was always at the bottom of the class.

His next school, called Brighton, was a more relaxed school run by two kindly ladies. In this school, his work was a bit better but still not good. He was known primarily for bad behaviour; the day he left the campus, the school declared a holiday.

Churchill attended a private school called Harrow where he was a poor student, succeeding only in fencing. At Harrow they lined up "in the order of their placement at the class."[1] Churchill was always last; his self-esteem suffered because he felt that everyone was better than he was.

"The Inhospitable Regions of Examinations"

Examinations were always a problem for Churchill. In an entrance examination for Harrow, when he was given a few paragraphs of Latin to translate, he only produced a large ink blot. He could not answer a single question in the Latin section. He stared at the page for two hours. He also did poorly on the examinations to get into Sandhurst, a military academy, and had to take the examinations three times to achieve a score high enough to be admitted. When he failed this examination the first time, he did do well in the English and history sections. The second time, he came closer to the grade required for entrance. Before the third try, he was sent to a special preparation coach called a "crammer." This time, he barely passed the examination; his score was not high enough to get into the infantry course but instead he entered the cavalry cadetship course.

Mathematics

Churchill tried desperately, but failed, to understand mathematics. He wrote that cosines, tangents, and square roots have "ugly faces." Commenting on the uselessness of the math he learned in school, he noted ironically that he had "never met any of these creatures since leaving."[2]

He speaks of descending into the "dismal bog called 'sums.'" As soon as he finished one calculation, there was another calculation—an endless parade of them. He struggled with arithmetic operations such as borrowing, which he claimed made his life difficult. The arithmetic operations put demands on working memory, and I suspect that Churchill's memory for numbers often failed him.

He received special tutoring in mathematics from a Mr. Mayo. Mr. Mayo "convinced me that Mathematics was not a hopeless bog of nonsense," and that with some tutoring and hard work, he might be able to make sense of it.[3]

Latin and Greek

Churchill believed that Latin was included in the curriculum to torment him. He preferred the simple and direct grammar of the English language. The complex structure of Latin and Greek presented him with a serious challenge. He sarcastically described the elaborate grammar of Latin and Greek as a way of "establishing posthumous fame" for these dead languages. For example, when his teacher explained that the vocative case meant the case that you should use in addressing a table, he correctly, but impertinently, said that he never spoke to tables. He was such a poor student that he was placed in the lowest form and did not have to learn much Latin or Greek, but they still presented their share of challenges.

In his four and half years at Harrow, translating Latin was always a problem. He found a fellow student who was good in Latin but not skilful at writing, and they worked out an exchange. Churchill wrote his compositions, and the student translated Churchill's Latin homework. They were almost caught when this student was quizzed on an essay that Churchill had written and the student did not answer questions very well.

He was so hopeless in Latin and Greek that the school decided that he should receive instruction in English composition instead of being forced to attend Latin and Greek classes. This instruction contributed to the development of the powerful speaking and writing style that was Churchill's trademark. Instead of "writing beautiful Latin poetry" and "pithy Greek epigrams," he learned how to write "powerful English sentences."

He liked history, poetry, and writing essays, but examinations were torture, especially in Latin and mathematics. In his view, "they always asked what I don't know," and he had no opportunity to display what he did know. He was not the first student, nor will he be the last, to say this. He thought languages should be introduced through history and the customs of the people who spoke the languages. He was ahead of his time; this approach to language teaching is called the communicative approach, which stresses understanding the meaning, rather than memorizing the grammar of the language.

Churchill envisioned a severe punishment for whoever decided that the pronunciation of Latin should not be like English. He maintained that schoolchildren should not be tortured with a foreign pronunciation. Since no one knows how Latin was actually pronounced, he did have a good point.

At Sandhurst, he learned map-making, military tactics, and other subjects relevant to the army. He was freed from the horrors of Latin, Greek, French, and mathematics.

Behavioural Problems

Churchill was a "troublesome boy." His report cards described him as careless, forgetful, late, and constantly losing things. By his own admission, and according to his teachers, he was very "naughty." One day, in a fit of defiant behaviour, he kicked his headmaster's straw hat to pieces; in another instance, he started a fight by pulling another boy's ear. He pushed a boy, fully clothed, into a stream. He almost drowned when he impetuously jumped off a boat and a storm came up suddenly.

But Churchill was also clever. It was the custom to step forward at the end of the day and report the number of demerits that one had received. When asked, he responded with "nine," an unusually high number even for the mischievous Churchill. "Number nine?" questioned one of his teachers. "The word I used was 'nein,' the German word for no," he responded. Like many children with learning disabilities, Churchill played the role of the class clown, and he certainly could make his classmates laugh.

One source of his behavioural problems may have been his learning disability. Winston was born two months prematurely and was sickly as a child. The types of difficulties he had with mathematics and attention frequently occur in premature babies.[4]

As a young child of seven, he was separated from his parents and sent to boarding school. Sad not to see his parents on a regular basis, Churchill wrote longingly about how much he looked forward to their visits, which were few and far between. His father was a Member of Parliament, and his parents attended numerous social events and spent time travelling to exotic locations without the young Winnie.

The schools that he attended were not like the Hogwarts of Harry Potter fame. There were no magic potions, flights on broomsticks, or solid doorways that one could slip through by saying a magic word. To us today, it may seem like a very difficult experience for a seven-year-old boy to be sent off to a boarding school. Emotional distress may have contributed to his behavioural problems.

On Schooling

Churchill described his school experiences as "an unhappy period in my life" and "a somber grey patch upon the chart of my journey."[5] School meant worries, discomfort, restriction, monotony, and discouragement. He described himself as a "backward school boy"—awkward and foolish at attempts at conversation with adults. His memories of school were bittersweet; he did develop some lifelong friendships that began at school, and he excelled at swimming and fencing. However, the good times and friends did not compensate for his suffering in school. In his autobiography he wondered, poignantly, whether we really need school at all.

Churchill was from a very wealthy family and had access to tutoring and extra help, but the failure to recognize his learning disability left emotional scars that he carried with him to his grave. Although he later became successful and respected all over the world, he never forgot his negative experiences in school.

Lessons Learned

There are lessons to be learned from Churchill's story. He provides us with some insights into how people with learning disabilities may acquire information. Churchill wrote about how much he liked lectures by experts, especially if they had a magic lantern show, the equivalent of contemporary slides, overheads, and PowerPoint. He could learn information not by rote memorization, but through logic, recounting of historical events, and visual images.

With Churchill, as with many children, an undiagnosed learning disability led to emotional pain, loss of self-esteem, and behavioural problems. Yet despite his disability, he was able to use his considerable talent for speaking and writing in the English language and achieved a place in history.

The Case of Paul—A Disability in Mathematics

Paul's parents brought him to me to be tested when he was eleven years old.[6] According to his parents, he was having "school work difficulties" and was "not trying." Paul's reading skills were quite good; he could quickly and accurately read complicated words such as *contagious*, *stratagem*, and *bibliography*. He could read unfamiliar made-up words such as *phintober*, *wroutch*, and *depmoniel* quite well, and he could read and pronounce words that he had never seen before. His score on a reading comprehension test, where he had to read passages and answer questions, was very good. He did not have dyslexia; however, he was still having serious problems in school because mathematics and spelling were a problem for Paul.

Paul struggled with the arithmetic problems that I gave him to solve. He was slow and inaccurate and did not know his multiplication tables or simple arithmetic facts. Figure 5 shows the types of errors Paul made.

EXAMPLES OF ERRORS

Basic Fact Errors

a)
$$\begin{array}{r} 6 \\ +2 \\ \hline 7 \end{array}$$

b)
$$\begin{array}{r} 75 \\ +8 \\ \hline 82 \end{array}$$

Sign Errors

c)
$$\begin{array}{r} 6 \\ +2 \\ \hline 4 \end{array}$$

d) $6 \div 2 = 12$

Place Value Errors

e)
$$\begin{array}{r} 75 \\ +8 \\ \hline 713 \end{array}$$

f)
$$\begin{array}{r} 452 \\ 137 \\ +245 \\ \hline 71214 \end{array}$$

Regrouping Errors

g)
$$\begin{array}{r} 401 \\ -74 \\ \hline 337 \end{array}$$

h)
$$6\overline{)968} \quad 111$$

Working Memory Errors

i)
$$\begin{array}{r} {}^{7}\;\;\; \\ 458 \\ +139 \\ \hline 651 \end{array}$$

j)
$$\begin{array}{r} 401 \\ -74 \\ \hline 323 \end{array}$$

Figure 5. Examples of Paul's arithmetic errors.

Students with mathematics disability have trouble remembering basic math facts. They make errors on simple calculations; sometimes they appear to ignore arithmetic signs and subtract when they should be adding or multiply when they should be dividing.

You can see what we call place value errors in examples (e) and (f) in Figure 5. It appears that Paul added the figures in each column without remembering that if the first column adds up to more than 10, you carry forward the additional number to the next column. To correctly do such calculations, you must be aware of what the columns for ones, tens, and hundreds mean. In example (e), estimation skills would have been helpful: 75 + 8 must be a number less than 100, not 713, as Paul wrote. In example (f), rounding the numbers (450 + 100 + 250) would give a total of about 800—certainly not more than the 70,000 Paul arrived at.

Paul did not understand regrouping (also known as carrying or borrowing), as you can see from the regrouping errors. Here again, estimation skills could have helped him with the answer. In example (h), if you understand that division is the opposite of multiplication and you multiply 6×111, the answer is 666 not 968, as Paul wrote. He did not think to check his work in this way.

Working memory is critical in mathematics. Working memory means that you draw on your knowledge, process incoming information, and remember at the same time. In example (i), when Paul added the first column, he knew that $8 + 9 = 17$, but he forgot the sequence and wrote the numbers 1 and 7 in the wrong places. The working memory errors shown in Figure 5 indicate how a problem with this basic process can result in completely wrong answers.

Paul's memory for numbers was poor, although his memory for words was good. On a spelling test he wrote the following words: *charicter* (character), *resonebel* (reasonable), and *mitirele* (material). The average person can decipher which words he wanted to write because he kept the correct sounds, but he did not represent them in the usual ways. As suggested previously, in English, unlike in some other languages, there are often many ways to write the same sound. How a particular English word is spelled depends on which language it derived from and/or what spelling conventions have developed over time.

Paul had trouble remembering what he read. He could talk about a story or a project, but he could not write down what he wanted to say. His spelling was terrible and his handwriting was messy. However, he drew very well and loved to act in school plays.

He struggled to learn French. Although his pronunciation was reasonably accurate, in doing dictation, he spelled almost every word incorrectly. He could not remember how to conjugate verbs or make subjects and verbs or adjectives and nouns agree, even after three years of French instruction in school.

The type of learning disability Paul had is developmental output failure or mathematics disability, first discussed in the previous chapter. People with this problem have difficulty with computational arithmetic and written work, and often with spelling. They also have problems with fine motor coordination and short-term memory, especially remembering numbers. People with this disability often have good oral language skills and a very good sense of humour; sometimes they are great mimics.

We can learn some lessons from this case study. A person can be good at solving problems and have excellent reasoning skills but still struggle with mathematics. One solution is for teachers to stress problem-solving and make sure that students understand the mathematical concept of place value and learn to estimate correct solutions and check simple calculations.

6

Hans Christian Andersen
A Case of Non-Verbal Learning Disability

An ugly duckling tormented by the other ducklings, ridiculed by children, rejected by his mother, turns into a beautiful swan. This lovely fairy tale, written by Hans Christian Andersen, is a classic and has found its way into the hearts of children and adults all over the world. Who can help but be delighted with the final triumph and immense happiness of the once "ugly" duckling?

Although the story is about ducks and swans, it is really a parable of the life of Andersen, a Danish writer and poet who was born in 1805 and died in 1875. Like the duckling that turned out to be a swan, Andersen was awkward, unattractive, and teased and scorned in the early part of his life.[1] He encountered many learning difficulties in school. But eventually, he achieved fame and recognition as a writer. His books and poems have been translated into over 150 different languages. He received honours from many countries, including, among others, Sweden, Mexico, Prussia, and, of course, his native Denmark. His statue stands in the Rosenborg Garden in Copenhagen.

The Ugly Duckling

Nothing in Andersen's early life foretold his eventual success. His family was very poor; his father was a cobbler and his mother was an illiterate washerwoman. As a child, her parents had forced her to beg on the street. Neither of his parents attended school. When his mother and father were children in the late eighteenth century, schools were not free, and often children were forced to work to help support the family.

Children teased the little boy, Hans Christian, because of his appearance. He had a big nose, small eyes, and a mop of unruly whitish-blond hair. He was tall and thin, even when he was a boy, and had very large hands and feet. He moved awkwardly. He was socially inept, telling his classmates wild and imaginative stories in which he was always the hero.

As a young boy and an adolescent, Hans Christian struggled in school. Some people claim he had dyslexia, but this is not accurate. He had no trouble learning to read, and read voraciously. He did, however, have a learning disability that caused him great difficulty with spelling, arithmetic, geography, Greek, and Latin. Hans Christian was always a poor speller. In school he was always afraid that the teacher would beat him to punish his bad spelling. He could not remember how to spell common words, he omitted silent letters, and he used the wrong vowels and deleted sounds or syllables. These types of spelling errors are characteristic of students with severe spelling problems. He wrote his first play at the age of sixteen, but it was full of spelling and grammar mistakes. His handwriting was hard to read. The letters he wrote contained many mistakes in spelling and syntax.

The Torture of School

Hans Christian hated Latin grammar and struggled to master it. A tutor gave him lessons in Latin so he could complete his education. When Hans Christian opened his Latin book, he was appalled by the declensions and conjugations. One of his biographers, Signe Toksvig, wrote that Hans Christian thought that grammar was very difficult and, when he was frightened, he complained that "the blood goes to my head and I answer wrongly."[2]

He had difficulty reading maps and memorizing material. When he was called on to recite, his classmates could feel the whole bench shake. German, French, geometry, Greek, Hebrew, history, geography, and even Danish were difficult for him. He describes himself as being overpowered by grammar, geography, and mathematics. He especially dreaded Greek and was devastated, but not surprised, when he received a low mark in that subject. He wrote that in school he felt like a "wild bird which is confined in a cage."[3]

Not surprisingly, Hans Christian was terrified of examinations. Before one examination he fainted, and before another he had a nosebleed. He prayed to God to make him smart enough to advance to the next grade in school. "He often used to pray for minor accidents in order to avoid a class with a teacher who tormented him."[4] His troubles with school made him consider suicide.

In her biography, *The Wild Swan: The Life and Times of Hans Christian Andersen*, Monica Stirling quotes Andersen's reflections on his school days: "The life I led comes back to me in bad dreams. Once again I sit in a fever on the school bench. I cannot answer, I dare not, and angry eyes stare at me, laughter and gibes echo around me."[5]

Some of his teachers became impatient with his difficulties. They teased him about his appearance, his awkwardness, and his "slowness." One teacher told him that he was a "stupid fellow" and nothing would ever come of him: "You'll scribble a lot, I have no doubt, when you are on your own but I don't imagine that anybody will ever read it; it will be sold for waste paper."[6]

Monica Stirling quotes Andersen as saying, "In school the rector took pleasure in mocking me, making fun of my person, and discussing my lack of talent."[7] According to another biographer, Rumer Godden, when Andersen left school, the schoolmaster who repeatedly humiliated him told him, "You will never become a writer. . . . Your verses will rot in a book-seller's attic and you will end your days in a mad house."[8]

From Ugly Duckling to Swan

Although some teachers mocked and humiliated Hans Christian, others took him under their wing and helped and encouraged him. These sensitive and caring teachers made a tremendous difference in his life. Over and over again, we see the enormous influence that teachers can have on the lives of people with learning disabilities. Praise and encouragement nourish self-concept but humiliation and blame destroy it.

Andersen blossomed when he received praise and encouragement. When he heard that a newspaper would publish two of his poems, he was thrilled. In 1829, he enjoyed considerable success with a published short story, and he also published a comedy and a collection of poems that season. Other books followed, including novels and travelogues. The first instalment of his immortal *Fairy Tales* (*Eventyr*, in Danish) was published in 1835. At the time of his death, he was an internationally renowned and treasured artist. He received a stipend from the Danish government as a "national treasure."

Non-Verbal Learning Disability

In hindsight, it seems likely that Hans Christian Andersen had a non-verbal learning disability, as well as spelling and mathematics learning disabilities. Non-verbal learning disability is similar in many ways to the mathematics disability described in chapter 5, yet different in some important ways. Like people with a mathematics disability, people with non-verbal learning disability can read and speak well, and often have a large vocabulary. They often have difficulty with spelling and with even very simple mathematical calculations. Their handwriting looks messy; the letters are uneven and all different sizes, and they cannot consistently write on a line.

Non-verbal learning disability, however, has some additional characteristics that are not in common with mathematics disability. People with this disability cannot judge the emotions expressed in facial expressions, tone of voice, or non-verbal gestures. They lack the ability to understand social situations. In a study by Tanya Galway and Jamie Metsala, elementary school-children were asked questions about a social situation such as the following: "You and Tom are friends. You have been assigned to work together on a science project in school and only have two days to finish the project. You meet after school and you say you want to start the project right away, but Tom wants to play softball first."[9] Compared to others, children with non-verbal disability were less likely to recognize emotions in themselves and others, had trouble understanding the viewpoint of the other people in the story, and were more likely to see others as hostile and mean.

Hans Christian Andersen lived in a dream world. He was a loner who rarely played with other boys. He had difficulty with social skills and described himself as "friendless." When he went to visit Charles Dickens, the Dickens family was appalled by Hans Christian's lack of sensitivity. According to the biographer Elias Bredsdorff, Sir Henry Dickens, the son of Charles Dickens, described Andersen as lovable and interesting but "strange," "somewhat of an oddity," and "gauche." The Dickens family enjoyed his thoughtfulness, imagination, and artistic paper cut-outs, but "the small boys in the family rather laughed at him behind his back."[10]

People with non-verbal disability may have a poor sense of rhythm and appear uncoordinated when doing athletic activities. They often have trouble completing even very simple visual-spatial tasks such as puzzles. Our understanding of this disability is not very developed, but we are gradually learning more about it.

7

Yeats, the Poet with Dyslexia

I know that I am very unhappy and have often said to myself, "When you grow up, never talk as grown-up people do of the happiness of childhood."

—William Butler Yeats

One can feel the anguish and sadness in these thoughts of the great Irish poet William Butler Yeats (1865–1939). The pain of his childhood permeates his autobiographical writings. One source of this pain was his dyslexia, although the concept of learning disabilities did not really exist when he was growing up and attending school in the late nineteenth century.

In his autobiography, Yeats writes frequently of the frustrations he experienced during his early school years. Yeats's spelling and punctuation skills were weak, his handwriting was often difficult to read, and he was not a strong academic student in most school subjects. Yet he became one of the major poets of the twentieth century, winning the Nobel Prize for literature in 1923.

Although his writing shows us the frustrations and self-doubts of one dyslexic, his story also illustrates his special talents, which many dyslexics possess.

Yeats had trouble learning to read. He wrote, "Several of my uncles and aunts had tried to teach me to read, and because they could not, and because I was much older than children who read easily, had come to think, as I have learnt since, that I had not all my faculties."[1] He felt that he was stupid because of his difficulties with reading. One of his biographers, A. Norman Jeffares, notes that Yeats "never learned to spell; to the end of his life he produced highly idiosyncratic versions of words, the best known being he puts 'suggar on his pares.'"[2] Furthermore, according to Jeffares, Yeats had some language difficulties and poor pronunciation; he divided up his words into "any amount of full stops where there weren't any."[3] These types of language difficulties are typical of people with dyslexia, although some dyslexics can be quite articulate and are fluent speakers.

Yeats was an admirer of Oscar Wilde; he was envious of Wilde's eloquence and his beautiful sentences, which seemed carefully crafted but were spontaneous. From Yeats's autobiography we get a sense of the frustration he felt in the early school years. His father tried to teach him to read but "was an angry and impatient teacher and flung the reading-book at my head."[4] Yeats thought of himself as lazy and so did his father and those who tried to teach him to read. Fortunately, his family did not give up on him. One of his biographers, R. F. Foster, wrote, "As JBY [William Butler Yeats's father] remembered it, the whole family tried to teach him to read, and became convinced he would never master it; all his life WBY would admit his blindness to grammar, spelling and the appearance of 'my lines up the paper.'"[5] Progress was very slow, and Yeats did not learn to read until well past the age when most children do.

Memory Difficulties

People with dyslexia have serious memory problems; Yeats was no exception: "I have remembered nothing that I read but only those things that I heard or saw."[6] Most dyslexics remember what they hear more easily and more accurately than what they read. Most would rather attend a lecture or see a film than read a book to learn about a topic.

He had trouble learning his schoolwork by heart: "I could not have learned a quarter of my night's work."[7] He complained that he had such difficulty learning his lessons that he was at the bottom of the class. With vivid imagery, he described trying to control his uncooperative thoughts: "When I tried to do anything with them, it was like trying to pack a balloon into a shed in a high wind."[8] Note the similarity to Susan Hampshire's description of the string inside her head in chapter 22. Both write about their reluctant brains that refused to co-operate when learning.

Yeats was, however, fascinated with oral language and able to recall it well. In his autobiography, he wrote that he derived a great deal of pleasure from listening to folk stories and poems. In school, he enjoyed geometry and algebra; numeracy and mathematics did not present any difficulties for him. Many people with dyslexia have no difficulty with mathematics. Yeats wrote, "I had always done Euclid easily, making the problems out while the other boys were blundering at the blackboard, and that often carried me from the bottom to the top of my class."[9]

Writing, on the other hand, was a serious problem. Yeats experienced difficulties writing essays as a student. "Sometimes we had essays to write. . . . I never got a prize, for the essays were judged by handwriting and spelling."[10] This is quite a startling statement from someone who subsequently won the Nobel Prize in literature. Yeats was to become a brilliant writer, but his talent was not recognized in school because his teachers saw only messy handwriting and many spelling mistakes. It is indeed sad that the teachers ignored the content and quality of what he wrote.

He had so much trouble with the memory work that was required in school that he devised this solution: "One day I had a lucky thought. A great many lessons were run through in the last hour of the day, things we had learnt or should have learnt by heart overnight, and not having known one of them for weeks, I cut off that hour without anybody's leave. I asked the mathematical master to give me a sum to work and nobody said a word."[11] Mathematics was easy for Yeats, and he used his skills in that area to avoid the subjects that were a problem for him. He chose to do mathematics rather than history and Latin. Mathematics involve problem solving and logical thinking; history and Latin involve memorization, which he dreaded. Avoidance of difficulties is quite common among people with learning difficulties; some develop very sophisticated strategies.

Yeats's literacy challenges even made him unable to write the entrance exams for Trinity College Dublin, a school that he really wanted to attend. This is quite surprising for someone who became a gifted writer. It illustrates that these types of examinations do not measure the potential of people with dyslexia, or perhaps of other students either.

School Difficulties

Yeats wrote, "I was unfitted for school work, and though I would often work well for weeks together, I had to give the whole evening to one lesson if I was to know it. . . . I was always near the bottom of my class, and always making excuses that but added to my timidity; but no master was rough with me." In the classroom, history lessons were "a column of seventy dates." He wrote, "I was worst of all at literature for we read Shakespeare for his grammar exclusively."[12]

Latin was difficult for Yeats. Speaking of his classmates, he said, "These boys had the same natural gift and instead of being in the fourth or fifth book were in the modern books at the end of the primer; and in place of a dozen lines of Virgil with a dictionary, I was expected to learn with the help of a crib a hundred and fifty lines. The other boys were able to learn the translation of, and to remember what words of Latin and English corresponded with one another, but I, who, it may be, had tried to find out what happened in the parts we had not read, made ridiculous mistakes."[13] Here we have some indication of his curiosity and interest, reading ahead to find out what happens, but also his struggles.

Problems with the French Language

People with dyslexia may experience problems when they try to learn a foreign language, especially when they are required to write, rather than speak, it. The young William Butler Yeats certainly did. He struggled with the grammar and the pronunciation of French. He would periodically take up French lessons throughout his life but found himself continually incapable of learning it or any other foreign language.

Visual Imagery

Dyslexia is a language disorder; thus, it may seem strange that a poet, whose work depends on the use of language, could have a language disorder. However, an examination of Yeats's poetry and prose reveals a series of vivid visual images, usually not arranged in a logical or sequential manner. There is rarely a play on words, and his work seems to lack the rich vocabulary that is characteristic of some other renowned prose and poetry. Yeats had a gift for visualizing and generating powerful images. Many individuals with dyslexia have above-average visualizing and visual memory skills in spite of relatively poor language skills, so Yeats's dyslexia may have influenced the type of poetry he wrote. In light of his dyslexia, Yeats may also have done a great deal of "stitching and unstitching," beyond the usual practice of poetic creation.

Self-Doubts

Yeats's slowness in reading and his misspellings, inaccurate punctuation, and sloppy handwriting are evidence of dyslexia. His autobiography is full of his childhood doubts and insecurities, characteristics that are often present in individuals with learning disabilities. At the beginning of his autobiography, Yeats quotes his great-uncle William Middleton as saying, "We should not make light of the troubles of children. They are worse than ours, because we can see the end of our trouble and they can never see any end." Reflecting on his own school troubles, Yeats writes, "I know that I am very unhappy. . . . There was no reason for my unhappiness. Nobody was unkind."[14] Yeats did not know that he had dyslexia; he was called "idle" because of his learning difficulties. He writes of his terror when confronted with schoolwork. A very real but then-unknown contributor to Yeats's unhappy childhood was his dyslexia.

Helping People with Dyslexia

The story of William Butler Yeats has also provided some insight into what might be a valuable technique to help individuals with learning disabilities. One of the basic tenets of Yeats's poetics was a theory based on a language of "personal utterance" and "the accumulated expression of the world." In his years of budding poetic genius, Yeats believed that "we should write out our own thoughts in as nearly as possible the language we thought them in, as though in a letter to an intimate friend. We should not disguise them in any way. . . . I tried from that on [*sic*] to write out of my emotions exactly as they came to me in life, not changing them to make them more beautiful."[15] From this personal statement, we gain important advice about how to design curriculum for students with learning disabilities. The most valuable text may be of the students' own creation, thus building self-esteem together with language skills. Allowing them to express their feelings is really important, not only for dyslexics but for all children.

The purpose of drawing attention to this disability in one of the great literary giants is to offer encouragement to those who presently endure the frustrations of these problems, and to illustrate through the achievements of an individual like Yeats that it is possible for those with dyslexia to go far beyond basic literacy.

Perhaps parents and teachers of children with dyslexia will be inspired by the brilliant accomplishments of someone who had dyslexia. Not all individuals with dyslexia need aspire to poetic greatness, but the possibility of achieving more than just a level of functional literacy may be well within their grasp.

PART II

History, Assessment, Diagnosis, and Misdiagnosis

8

Jane Austen
The First Educational Psychologist

The description of learning disabilities began not with scientists but with fiction writers whose keen observations of human behaviour recognized learning disabilities long before the scientific and educational communities understood they existed. Of course, fiction writers did not label what they wrote about as "learning disabilities," but they described the conditions as well as any contemporary textbook or scientific study—perhaps even better.

The first person to recognize learning disabilities was the novelist Jane Austen, who in 1798 described a child who appears to have dyslexia in her ironic novel *Northanger Abbey*. In this novel, Austen paints a picture of a young girl who had a variety of learning difficulties and helps us understand the gifts, as well as the problems, of children who struggle with learning. The idea of learning disabilities would not exist for another 150 years; however, Austen observed human behaviour and wrote about what she saw with insights similar to those of contemporary educational psychologists.

The central character in *Northanger Abbey* is Catherine Morland. "No one who had ever seen Catherine Morland in her infancy, would have supposed her born to be a heroine."[1]

Catherine was not a willing reader. "It was not very wonderful that Catherine, who had by nature nothing heroic about her, should prefer cricket, base ball, riding horseback, and running about the country at the age of fourteen, to books."[2] Today we would call Catherine dyslexic, or a "reluctant reader" or "struggling reader." In Austen's words, "Writing and accounts she was taught by her father; French by her mother: her proficiency in either was not remarkable, and she shirked her lessons in both whenever she could."[3]

An accomplished young woman of that time was expected to be fluent in French. Catherine clearly was not. She demonstrated the difficulties with foreign languages that are so common in people with learning disabilities. Learning a foreign language involves a great deal of rote memory. Memory problems are characteristic of a learning disability, as they were with Catherine. "She never could learn or understand any thing before she was taught; and sometimes not even then, for she was often inattentive and occasionally stupid. Her mother was three months in teaching her only to repeat the 'Beggar's Petition,' and after all, her next sister, Sally, could say it better than she did."[4] To the horror of the society matrons of her time, Catherine was unable to write beautiful and polished sonnets.

In addition to problems with mathematics, French, and memory, Catherine struggled with handwriting, as do children with a writing disability. "Her greatest deficiency was in the pencil—she had no notion of drawing."[5] Catherine's artistic productions were not the delicate and exquisite ones expected of young ladies. "Her taste for drawing was not superior; though whenever she could obtain the outside of a letter from her mother, or seize upon any other odd piece of paper, she did what she could in that way, by drawing houses and trees, hens and chickens, all very much like one another."[6]

Catherine was also a failure at learning music. "Her mother wished her to learn music; and Catherine was sure she should like it, for she was very fond of tinkling the keys of the old forlorn spinet; so, at eight years old she began. She learnt a year and could not bear it; and Mrs. Morland, who did not insist on her daughters being accomplished in spite of incapacity or distaste, allowed her to leave off. The day that they dismissed the music-master was one of the happiest of Catherine's life."[7]

Catherine could not play music, but in today's jargon, she was a "good listener." Jane Austen writes, "Though there seemed to be no chance of her throwing a whole party into raptures by a prelude on the pianoforte, of her own composition, she could listen to other people's performance with very little fatigue."[8]

Behavioural Problems

Catherine had some behavioural problems. "She was moreover noisy and wild, hated confinement and cleanliness, and loved nothing so well in the world as rolling down the green slope at the back of the house. . . . She was fond of all boys' plays, and greatly preferred cricket not merely to dolls, but to the more heroic enjoyments of infancy, nursing a dormouse, feeding a canary-bird, or watering a rose-bush. Indeed she had no taste for a garden; and if she gathered flowers at all, it was chiefly for the pleasure of mischief—at least so it was conjectured from her always preferring those which she was forbidden to take."[9] Impulsively plucking flowers from a garden is a behaviour that we might see in a child with an attention deficit.

Although Austen did not intend to write a case study in *Northanger Abbey*, she provided a remarkable description of a girl with learning problems. It seems reasonable to infer that her fictional heroine, Catherine Morland, had dyslexia. Austen writes about Catherine with affection and exasperation. These conflicting emotions mirror the feelings of every parent or teacher of a child with a learning disability. I have read and written hundreds of case studies. With every one that I read or write, I harbour a secret wish that we professionals could write in the style of Jane Austen. What fun it would be to read such case studies.

Austen's Insights

Jane Austen was not a psychologist, educator, pediatrician, psychiatrist, learning disabilities specialist, speech therapist, or social worker. Or, perhaps, she was all of these. We can be justifiably proud of the advances made in the understanding and treatment of learning disabilities in the past forty or so years, but Jane Austen, a keen observer of the human condition and a great writer, identified these difficulties in the late eighteenth century.

Jane Austen was not the only writer who scooped the scientists. George Eliot, writing about sixty years after Jane Austen, has written a remarkable description of a dyslexic. The next chapter discusses Eliot's "case study."

9

"Stupid Tom"
George Eliot on Dyslexia

A boy named Tom prayed, "Please make me remember my Latin. And make Mr. Stelling say that I shan't do Euclid any more."

—George Eliot

Tom Tulliver is the remarkable creation of the novelist George Eliot (1819–1880), who wrote about him in 1860 in *The Mill on the Floss*. Similar to Jane Austen, George Eliot used her keen powers of observation to develop a central character who was dyslexic. Eliot's sympathetic and compelling portrait of a dyslexic was written almost forty years before any cases of dyslexia were described in the medical literature and a hundred years before the word *dyslexia* was commonly used in the English language. Her depiction of dyslexic Tom is as accurate as if she had read accounts of dyslexia in medical journals.

George Eliot is the pen name of Mary Ann Evans, a woman forced to write using a man's name because women writers were not taken seriously. In that era, the common belief was that women could write only romances and "silly novels," not literary and intelligent ones.

In Eliot's novel, Tom's father describes his son in these words: "But he's slow with his tongue, reads quite poorly and can't abide the books and spells all wrong."[1] This is a chillingly accurate picture of a dyslexic. Except for the phrasing, it could have been written today. Similar to dyslexics through the centuries, Tom struggled with reading, spelling, and grammar. Latin and geometry left him bewildered. He sometimes had difficulty pronouncing words, understanding the subtleties of language, and finding the correct word.

Tom had difficulty learning to read and hated reading. "Oh, but I don't like reading; I sooner have you tell them me. But only the fighting ones you know."[2] Tom did not want to hear any "girls' stories"; he relished stories about battles and conquering heroes, stories of conflict like David and Goliath and Samson. He wanted someone to tell him the stories, rather than having to read them. Similar to many people with dyslexia, Tom's memory and understanding of what he heard was good, but reading was a struggle.

In today's educational system, we try to teach dyslexic children and adults with books that are about subjects that interest them, from ballet dancing to dinosaurs to mountain biking to reggae and all sorts of other topics. George Eliot had the insight to recognize that people with dyslexia could be taught to read more easily with books on subjects that are interesting and meaningful to them. This may seem obvious now, but it certainly was not educational practice 150 years ago. Even today, we do not always provide struggling readers with stimulating books.

Tom had ample opportunity to learn to read. Filled with aspirations for his son, Tom's father sent him away to school so he could get a good education and learn to argue with the lawyers that tormented Mr. Tulliver. He wanted Tom to do the accounts and help in the family business.

Unfortunately, schooling for Tom was not a success. Geometry and grammar were nearly impossible for him. Tears of frustration dimmed his eyes when he tried to study; he hated crying and was ashamed of it but he could not help it. In school he felt inadequate for the first time in his life.

Tom's teacher, Mr. Stelling, did not understand him. Eliot wrote, "Besides, it was the fault of Tom's mental constitution that his faculties could not be nourished with the sort of knowledge Mr. Stelling had to communicate. A boy born with a deficient power of apprehending signs and abstractions must suffer the penalty of his congenital deficiency, just as if he had been born with one leg shorter than the other."[3] Mr. Stelling "was convinced that a boy so stupid at signs and abstractions must be stupid at everything else."[4] Tom's teacher used the "thumb screw method": each subsequent exercise should be harder and judged more severely. Eventually Mr. Stelling relaxed a bit and Tom learned better, but never really well. Tom clearly did not suit the educational system of the day. Mr. Stelling thought that Tom was intentionally refusing to learn, did not care, and had no interest. He could not have been more wrong.

Not surprisingly, Tom longed to escape from school. When Tom's father visited him at boarding school, he told Tom that he looked well and that school agreed with him. Tom secretly wished that he had looked ill, anything to escape from the prison of the school building and the interminable lessons. Although Tom was robust and healthy, he begged his father to take him out of the school because his schoolwork "brings on the toothache."

The toothache was imaginary, but Tom was aware of his difficulties and tried, unsuccessfully, to cope with them.

Tom's teacher attributed the problem to Tom's lack of interest in what he was doing, carelessness, and laziness. Mr. Stelling did not see Tom's abilities; he saw only his failure to understand grammar and geometry: "He was in the state bordering on interest idiocy with regard to the demonstration that two different triangles must be equal." Eliot writes, "He could discern with great promptitude and certainty the fact that they were equal," but his teacher did not recognize Tom's visual skills. Tom was ridiculed and called an idiot because of his troubles at school.[5]

Like many people with dyslexia, Tom sometimes had difficulty understanding the more subtle aspects of language, and he was the victim of being teased about it. Once when there was a delicious roast beef on the table, Mr. Stelling asked him whether he wanted to "decline" the roast beef or Latin. Hating Latin, Tom mistakenly answered the roast beef, because he did not understand the double meaning of "decline."

Cultivating the Mind

Tom's teacher believed that subjects such as Latin and geometry would train and prepare the mind, serving as a sort of mental gymnastics. "Mr. Stelling concluded that Tom's brain, peculiarly impervious to etymology and demonstrations, was particularly in need of being ploughed and harrowed by these patent instruments: it was his favorite metaphor, that the classics and geometry constituted a culture of the mind which prepared it for the reception of any subsequent crop."

George Eliot turned the metaphor on its head. She wrote, "Call the brain an intellectual stomach" and imagine that Tom had been plied with "cheese in order to remedy a gastric weakness, which prevented him from digesting it."[6] In other words, just giving him more of what he could not do would not correct the problem. This insightful comment is still relevant today. Often, we force children to do drills in whatever subject gives them difficulty, rather than structuring the learning so they can understand it. George Eliot seemed to grasp that Tom had some sort of weakness that could not be cured by inflicting more and more Latin and geometry.

Tom resorted to prayer, praying for the ability to do his schoolwork. Tom's prayers echo the sentiments of many children struggling with learning problems. Sometimes Tom's prayers were answered for a day and he could learn his Latin lesson; unfortunately, the solution was only temporary because by the following day he had forgotten what he had learned the day before.

Recognizing Special Abilities

Tom's teacher did not appreciate Tom's gifts: his perceptual discrimination abilities, his skill in estimating length and distance, and his ability to draw accurately. Tom could predict with accuracy "what number of horses were cantering behind him, he could throw a stone right into the centre of a given ripple, he could guess to a fraction how many lengths of his stick it would take to reach across the playground, and could draw almost perfect squares on his slate without any measurement."[7] Today we would call these perceptual and visual-spatial abilities. Tom was also skilled at active games and making fishing tackle, whipcord, rabbit pens, and gate handles. Maggie, his sister, who was a great reader, was impressed by his knowledge of worms.

George Eliot recognized the type of skills that are really strong in many people with dyslexia. It was as if she had an implicit understanding of multiple intelligences, a concept made popular by Howard Gardner.[8] Gardner proposed that there is not one kind of general intelligence, but several dimensions of intelligence, from verbal to mathematics, visual, musical, sensitivity to the emotions of others, and self-awareness. We all have these dimensions of intelligence, but certain people have outstanding abilities in some areas. George Eliot's novel *The Mill on the Floss* captures the remarkable variation in human abilities. Along with Tom, the character of rebellious Maggie is totally believable, and is said to be George Elliot's alter ego.

Similar to all parents of children with learning problems, Tom's parents tried to solve the puzzle of his difficulties, especially given that his sister could read so well. Tom's father speculated that the reason for Tom's slowness was that he took after his wife's family. His wife agreed and noted, "He's wonderful for liking a deal o' salt in his broth. That was my brother's way, and my father's before him."[9] There is, of course, no connection between salt preference and dyslexia, but today we know that dyslexia runs in families and has a genetic basis. Tom's father had difficulty reading and did not like it. Mr. Tulliver only bought books if they had "handsome bindings." Eliot's use of this folk wisdom in her writing predates the research on the genetics of dyslexia by almost a hundred years.

Maggie

Tom's learning difficulties are in sharp contrast to his sister Maggie's desire to read and learn. Maggie "could read almost as well as the parson" and better than most adults. [10] Had she been a boy and been educated, she would have been, according to her father, "a match for the lawyers."[11] Mr. Tulliver hated lawyers because he lost his property due to a legal decision against him.

As a child, Maggie's nose was always in a book, and when asked, she could give an "eloquent discourse" about the books she read. She was a proselytizer for reading. She was eager to share books with Luke, the head worker at the mill, who confessed that he was "no reader" and never read any books but the Bible (and not much of that). Maggie wanted Luke to read a book about the people of Europe, but he was not interested in knowing about them, claiming that books distract men from their work and making a living.

Like Luke, Tom had little interest in reading. He thought that Maggie was a silly girl. She could not throw a stone to hit anything, could not do tricks with a pocket knife, and was frightened of frogs.

Insights about Dyslexia

George Eliot wrote with compassion and sensitivity about dyslexia. She understood the abilities, as well as the struggles, of people with dyslexia. Her portrait of Tom is so accurate that it is difficult to believe that he was not a real person. How did she develop these insights? In real life, Mary Ann Evans's father was not much of a speller; perhaps there was some dyslexia in the family. There is also speculation, but no evidence one way or the other, that her brother Isaac was dyslexic. Her portrait of the dyslexic Tom is so knowledgeable and sympathetic that it stands as a remarkable testament to her powers of observation, her comprehension, and her compassion.

10

The Scientific Discovery
of Dyslexia

In 1896, Percy, a fourteen-year-old boy, walked into the office of W. Pringle Morgan, an ophthalmologist in Sussex, England.[1] Dr. Morgan was puzzled by Percy, a boy who was intelligent but who could not learn to read or spell in spite of seven years of effort by his teachers. Percy's problem was a perplexing case: he was "a bright and intelligent boy, quick at games," but he could not learn to read or spell. Although the term did not exist at the time, this case was the first example of dyslexia in a child that was described in the scientific literature.

Morgan labelled Percy's condition "congenital word blindness." This rather intriguing label gives us a clue to what he thought the problem was. He believed that the root of dyslexia was the inability to remember what words look like, a lack of visual memory for words. This observation has stood the test of time. People who had this condition seemed to be unable to read words, as if they were blind. It was congenital because it was present from birth, not the result of a lack of education. Morgan believed, correctly, it was due to inadequate development of a part or parts of the brain.

When Morgan dictated words to Percy, the responses were clearly incorrect. For example, for *song* Percy wrote *scone*, for *subject* he wrote *scojock*, for *English* he wrote *Englis*, for *without* he wrote *wichout*, and for *seashore* he wrote *seasow*. These errors indicate that Percy had a speech perception problem because he could not adequately perceive *sh* or *th* sounds and could not easily write the *b* sound.

Percy stumbled over the reading and spelling of words, except for simple words such as *and, the,* and *of,* but he could read numbers very well. He could do arithmetic calculations easily, but he could not solve arithmetic problems because he could not read the words. Morgan reported that written words "have no meaning to him." Yet, "his schoolmaster, who taught him for some years, said that he would be the smartest lad in the school if the instruction were entirely oral."[2]

Ironically, more than a hundred years ago, Morgan foreshadowed what would become an important means of instruction years later. He recognized that children can learn orally, and that although reading is important, it is not the only way to learn about the world. Today, we encourage the use of films, videos, charts, maps, and illustrations to help people who have reading problems learn concepts.

Morgan was optimistic that a child with severe reading problems could be helped by instruction. Initially, Percy could not learn his letters; he was, in Morgan's words, "letter blind," but by instruction and hard work he did learn his letters, although it is not clear whether he ever became a fluent reader.

In the early 1900s, James Hinshelwood, a Scottish ophthalmologist, published a number of cases of "word blindness."[3] He described a case of a thirteen-year-old boy who could not read after seven years in school. The boy was good at drawing and "fair" at arithmetic. He could remember much of what he heard, but did not know all the letters of the alphabet. He had been taught by the "look and say" method, which teaches children to memorize words as if they were pictures, without learning the sounds of the letters of the alphabet. Hinshelwood recommended that children with "word blindness" should be taught reading individually, not with an entire class, so as not to experience ridicule by other children. How right he was! He also recommended short lessons every day rather than long ones, another observation that is consistent with today's approach to working with children with learning problems.

All the children Hinshelwood described were intelligent but had severe problems with reading, which he believed were caused by problems with visual memory. They were all good at arithmetic. He described one fifty-year-old man who could not learn to read but would always bring back the correct change when he was sent to pay a bill. Some of the children Hinshelwood tested had good auditory memories and could remember stories if they heard them. Many were slow to learn to speak. In most cases, there was a family history of reading problems, suggesting a genetic basis.

Hinshelwood recognized that children differ in the severity of their reading problems. He stated firmly that we should not treat these children and adults as imbeciles. Foreshadowing contemporary ideas, he encouraged teachers to use a variety of senses in teaching reading. He recognized that progress in reading would be slow but was possible with remediation.

These early pioneers in the field of learning disabilities questioned whether children with reading disabilities were just "fools"—was the problem really low intelligence? Demonstrating a wisdom that is sometimes absent today, they reasoned that if a child understood and spoke language well and could identify objects, intelligence was not the issue. Furthermore, if the child was competent at arithmetic and could write numbers, and appeared to have normal social behaviour, he or she did not lack intelligence. Therefore these pioneers of learning disabilities did not need expensive and time-consuming intelligence tests to distinguish between low intelligence and reading disability. It is interesting to note that physicians were instrumental in identifying dyslexia; educators were silent. Until the 1970s, learning disabilities remained in the hands of physicians.

All of the early reports noted that learning disabilities were more common in boys than girls. However, we now know that almost as many girls have dyslexia. Boys are more likely to be referred for assessment because they misbehave in school, but in large samples of children, girls are almost as likely to be dyslexic. Through the centuries, girls were not expected to be successful in school, so if they were quiet but could not read, they did not get noticed or tested for learning disabilities.

The Pioneering Work of Samuel Orton

Samuel Orton, a US neuropathologist and psychiatrist, was a pioneer in the field of learning disabilities.[4] During the 1920s, he recognized that some children whom teachers called "dull, subnormal or failing or retarded in schoolwork" were not stupid but merely had severe difficulty in learning to read and write. In Hinshelwood's words, they had "congenital word blindness." Orton gave this condition the name *strephosymbolia*, which means "twisted symbols." He reported that children with this condition left out letters when writing words; for example, one boy wrote *dierom* for *dining room*, *supr* for *supper*, and *blak* for *black*. Note that in some cases if you say these misspellings out loud, they sound very similar to the correct word. This is very common with dyslexics. Sometimes the children wrote letters backwards or wrote *b* in place of *d*, and vice versa. This confusion is not a visual problem; it is a problem of remembering the names of the letters. Letter reversal and transposing letters became the basis for the widely held, but incorrect, belief that dyslexia involves reading and writing backwards.

Samuel Orton was preoccupied with whether these children's reading problems stemmed from low intelligence. However, he ruled this out because they could recognize and name objects and they understood passages that were read to them. He challenged IQ tests as a valid basis for measuring intelligence because of the memory and language requirements of the test. Unlike many of his colleagues and some professionals today, he understood that scores on intelligence tests do not fairly reflect intellectual capacity. He reported the case of one boy, M.P., age sixteen, who had a low score on the IQ test. This boy could not visualize words and recognize them in print. Orton tested his theory about the inadequacy of IQ tests by asking M.P. questions concerning the adjustment of bearings in a V-type engine. (Those of us with a mechanical skill disability cringe at this question.) M.P. answered quickly and with obvious ability. This question required "good visualizing power for [the] answer, and his replies were prompt and keen." [5] When Orton gave M.P. tests that required mechanical skill, his performance was in the superior range.

Yet M.P. had extreme difficulties with reading and writing. He could name the letters of the alphabet but not say their sounds. His written composition was a jumble of words that made no sense, although in conversation his responses were direct and meaningful. His spelling errors were typical of much younger children and dyslexic readers: *fifteen* was read as *fighting*, *child* as *chailled*. *Strange* was spelled as *standard*, *nice* as *nike*, and *fellow* as *flyne*.

M.P. would reverse parts of a word; for example, he spelled *dug* as *gud*, *gray* as *gary*, or he would know the first sound and guess the rest, such as reading *blue* as *black* or *blow*. He also confused vowels, reading *bell* as *ball*. He told Orton that he was unable to remember the spelling of words because "it takes me so long that by the time I read them, I forget what was ahead of them."[6]

Orton reported that most of the children with reading and writing disabilities were delayed in learning to talk and were clumsy. Most were co-operative and anxious to please, but they all felt inferior because of their reading problems. Orton obviously felt compassion for these children, and he tried to teach them to read, but was unsuccessful in his brief attempts. He was against the so-called "look and say" method and suggested that they be taught with phonics, learning the sound of the letters, which is still the most popular method today. One of the most common methods of teaching phonics today bears his name, the Orton-Gillingham method.

The Evolution of Learning Disability Theories

All of the early pioneers in the field of learning disabilities recognized that problems with certain areas of the brain were causing the reading and writing difficulties. However, during the 1950s and 1960s, many social workers, psychologists, and psychiatrists blamed the families, especially the mothers, for their children's reading problems.[7] The brain disappeared from the equation. The children were considered scapegoats, victims of turmoil within the family. The mothers, rarely the fathers, were the perpetrators of children's reading problems. The mothers were labelled "non-nurturing, controlling, and seductive." There was no analysis of the children's reading difficulties, and few attempts to help them.

Fortunately, the late 1960s and 1970s witnessed a rapid growth in understanding learning disabilities. Another pioneer in the field was Samuel Kirk, who coined the term "learning disabilities" in 1963. He defined learning disabilities as "a retardation, disorder, or delayed development in one or more of the processes of speech, language, reading, writing, arithmetic or other school subject resulting from a psychological handicap caused by a possible cerebral dysfunction and/or emotional or behavioral disturbances. It is not the result of mental retardation, sensory deprivation, or cultural and instructional factors."[8]

This definition marked the beginning of the attempt to generalize and codify the idea of learning disabilities. Over the past fifty years, our knowledge of learning disabilities has grown dramatically, although we have not solved all the mysteries. Unfortunately, the sad fact is that we do not always put our knowledge into practice in schools.

11

Tiptoeing through the Minefield of Diagnosis

Diagnosing a learning disability is like entering a minefield.[1] You must navigate around long-held myths, trip over cherished beliefs, stumble over unsubstantiated assumptions, and invade closely guarded professional territory. You meet hostile attitudes at every turn.

There are seemingly endless debates about what to call learning disabilities and how to define them. Some educators resist the term *dyslexia* and want the problem to be called a reading disability. Some think learning disabilities should be called *learning difficulties* or *learning differences*. In fighting about the name, professionals often overlook the people with the problem.

There is also controversy about whether people should be identified as learning disabled. Parents and teachers sometimes think that having the label dyslexic or learning disabled will make a child give up and not try, or become sad or angry. The reverse is the case; the label helps the person understand the problem. In their own words, here are some responses to the issue of labelling, from people with learning disabilities.

> It had a name; I wasn't stupid, the psychologist said I wasn't stupid and it was a lovely feeling. I thought, I can probably get some form of help and carry on studying and do what I want to do. I actually had a sense of purpose for the first time, which was wonderful.

> I thought at least I'm not as stupid as I thought I was.

> Sometimes it's better to know you're dyslexic than not to know it. At least I know it's not me being stupid.

> It made me think it wasn't my fault anyway, it's something in my head, even though I wasn't totally sure what it meant.

> I feel better knowing I'm dyslexic.

> It's a good thing to actually be labelled it than not labelled it, because you've still got the same problems whether labelled or not. It's perceived in a better way knowing you're dyslexic than not knowing you're dyslexic.

> I'd rather not be dyslexic, but I am dyslexic and it's better knowing.

> I remember after I had seen the educational psychologist I got the results back. It was like a massive weight had lifted off my shoulders and suddenly I wasn't stupid anymore.

The same theme echoes throughout these comments: it is better to have a label, something concrete to help people with learning disabilities understand the problem.

Being labelled with a learning disability is not an excuse. In my role as an educational psychologist, when I tested an eleven-year-old boy and told him he had dyslexia, and explained what it was, he said, "Does this mean I don't have to clean up my room?" The simple answer is an emphatic *no*. Dyslexia is not an excuse for failing to take out the garbage, for not cleaning up your room, or for not helping with household chores.

Why is it helpful if people receive the diagnosis of learning disability or dyslexia? Most children know that something is the matter long before they are diagnosed, and many of their parents also suspect something is wrong. Sometimes when parents attempt to tell school authorities that their child has a problem, they are called over-anxious and told that the child is lazy, not very capable, or just badly behaved. "My mother had a real fight on her hands to get me tested," said one student with a learning disability. "The labelling was a relief."

Finding the Real Learning Disability

How do we know who has a learning disability? You would think the answer to that question would be simple, but it is not. We need to do educational testing to determine if a person has a learning disability, and this takes time. One frustrated mother asked me, "Can't you just do a blood test?" Unfortunately, there is no blood test or thermometer that measures whether someone has a learning disability. Measuring learning disabilities is not like measuring height or weight or broken bones. When the measuring device is a tape measure or a scale or an X-ray, there is agreement on what the results show. Unfortunately, this is not the case with tests for learning disabilities.

Learning disabilities are not real entities; there is no area of the brain where you can point to a learning disability. Identifying a learning disability is more like defining obesity than diagnosing measles. If you have a rash that is typical of measles and a fever, cough, and other common symptoms, a physician will diagnose you with measles. If a man is 170 centimetres (5 feet 7 inches) tall and weighs 200 kilograms (440 pounds), then he is considered obese. But if the same man were to weigh 100 kilos (220 pounds), is he overweight or obese? There is not a clear line between the two. So it is with learning disabilities. Where do you draw the line between normal achievement and a learning disability?

One of the major reasons that we often still fail to identify learning disabilities is the preoccupation with testing that dominates the field. We have made the identification process too time-consuming and irrelevant to the educational needs of learning-disabled children and adults. Typically, there is a long wait, often as long as two years, which is a very long time if you are an eight-year-old having problems with reading. In order for a child to be identified and given assistance within our school system, it has become the usual practice to administer many tests, sometimes in five- to six-hour sessions or spread over two days. Usually an IQ test is required, despite evidence that this is not necessary and does not guide remediation in a meaningful way. Often a psychologist writes a report of forty or more single-spaced pages, called a psychoeducational report, which contains numerous test results and lots of jargon but very little advice on how to help the person. One of the difficulties with excessive reliance on psychoeducational testing is that remediation is often neglected. That is, there is no attempt to relate the test scores to what educational methods and strategies might be used to help the child.

Some psychologists argue vehemently for this type of intensive testing for learning disabilities. Such tests may provide interesting information, but I argue that they are not necessary for diagnosis. For those brave enough to enter the minefield, it is possible to diagnose learning disabilities with a simple system that I will describe below. The professionals have made diagnosis complicated, but it really is not.

Diagnosis

Learning disabilities are defined as significant difficulties in reading, spelling, computational arithmetic, mathematics, and/or writing in spite of average or above-average intelligence.[2] Learning disabilities are limited to domains that have to do with school learning—specifically, reading, writing, spelling, arithmetic calculation, and mathematical problem-solving. Of course, it is possible to have a great deal of trouble learning to drive a car, become proficient at downhill skiing, develop a good backhand in tennis, play the piano, sing on key, and/or dance without stepping on your partner's feet, but these are not what we mean when we speak of learning disabilities.

A learning disability does not result from lack of educational opportunity, mental retardation, severe behavioural and emotional problems, or sensory impairment. If a person is blind or deaf, obviously that will have an impact on learning, but this is not considered a learning disability. If a child is locked in a closet for several years, the resulting failure to read, spell, or do mathematics is not a learning disability. If a person has very severe emotional and/or behavioural problems, these difficulties may interfere with learning, but they do not cause a learning disability. In fact, emotional difficulties and social problems at school are often a result of undiagnosed learning disabilities.

We measure learning disabilities through testing. Tests of word recognition, decoding (pseudoword reading), spelling, writing, mathematical problem-solving and computational arithmetic will detect most learning disabilities. A low score on any of these tests is a danger signal and usually means the person has a learning disability. There are an almost infinite number of tests available, but more detailed testing should not be done without considering what the tests really tell us.

The purpose of testing is to identify the learning disability or disabilities and to help decide on techniques that may help the person. Basic testing should be done routinely, starting in grade 1. I do not recommend the so-called high stakes testing, testing that is given to groups of students and usually does not measure basic skills very well. I advocate individually administered tests that can be done in approximately forty-five minutes.

Testing for Reading Skills

In assessing reading skills, we need to examine two processes: the ability to read words automatically, and the ability to sound out words. Assessing an individual for the possibility of dyslexia must include a measure of word reading, called word recognition skills. In tests of word reading, the person reads a list of words out loud, such as *book* or *cat* or *contradictory* or *valedictorian*. The words gradually increase in difficulty. By comparing an individual's reading skills to normal expectations for other people of the same age, we can determine whether or not the reading skills are average, below average, or above average. Word-reading skills are the building blocks and the basis of understanding print, so it is important to know if skills in this area are significantly below average.

As I discussed in chapter 2, we also measure how a person reads what are called pseudowords, pronounceable combinations of letters that are not real words but can be pronounced according to the rules of English. This type of test is essential to identify difficulties a person may have in associating letters and sounds, which is the key to decoding words in an alphabetic language like English. In addition to knowing how accurately an individual reads words and pseudowords, we also need to know how quickly he or she reads. If reading speed is too slow, comprehension will be difficult, and the person will forget the beginning of the paragraph, or even the sentence, before reaching the end. In a typical test of reading speed, called reading fluency, the individual must read as many words or pseudowords as possible in forty-five seconds.

The test of how well a person understands what he or she is reading is called reading comprehension. We test this by having a person read sentences and paragraphs and then answering multiple-choice questions about them. Assessing reading comprehension is more complex than assessing reading of single words or pseudowords, and performance on such tests may be influenced by many factors. For example, sometimes questions can be answered without reading the text. Consider the following question adapted from a standardized reading comprehension test. "Mangoes are not grown in which of the following places: Central America, South America, India, or the North Pole?" Even without reading the test paragraph about growing mangoes, many people probably know the answer.

Reading comprehension tests usually must be completed

in a certain amount of time. Slow readers may understand what they read, but they are penalized on tests with time limits because they may not have time to finish the test. People also use different strategies for recalling information, and this affects how they score on timed tests. A person who recalls information about a story will likely have a faster response time than someone who cannot recall the information but can remember its spatial location and look back quickly. And the latter person will have a faster response time than a person who cannot remember anything about a passage and has to search throughout it to answer questions.

Sometimes reading comprehension tests require the person to read a passage out loud. Because there are clues to the meaning of words from the surrounding context, it can be difficult to assess whether the person is reading each word or guessing the word based on the context. As well, some people have difficulty reading out loud and remembering at the same time, so they cannot answer the comprehension questions if they have to read a passage out loud. An individual's performance on a reading comprehension test is also influenced by familiarity with the subject matter. For example, some people would understand more of a passage about hockey or football; others would find reading about ballet or Baroque music much easier. Therefore, it is important to consider all the requirements of reading tests when looking at reading comprehension scores.

Phonological Awareness and Spelling

Phonological awareness, the ability to listen to speech and break it down into smaller segments, is a basic skill needed for reading. We measure phonological awareness by asking a person to do a variety of tasks such as to say *pink* without the *p* (when we think of *p*, we say the sound, not the letter) or *helicopter* without the *cop*. If people can successfully do this task, they isolate the sound in the word from the other sounds. Another task is what we call blending, where individuals hear the sounds, not the letters, in a word like *c – a – t*, and they have to blend them together to say the word. In a task called segmentation, we say a word and ask them to say each individual sound within that word. So if they hear the word *like*, they have to say the *l* sound, the long *i* sound, and the sound of *k*.

People who have difficulty spelling usually have some kind of learning disability; therefore, a test of dictation words should also be included in the assessment for learning disabilities. To determine the level of spelling, we compare the person's score on the spelling test with the scores of other people of the same age.

There are different kinds of spelling errors.[3] Consider the word *nature*. It could be misspelled as *natur* or *nachure*. The latter spelling shows that the individual has a good idea of the sounds in the word but not how to represent them with letters. The former shows that the person has a good visual image of the word but does not understand how the English language represents the sounds in the word. In order to understand a person's spelling strategies, we need to determine what kind of errors they make. Then remediation can be provided.

Testing for Writing Skills

Like reading comprehension testing, testing for writing skills can be complex. Writing involves two types of skills: composition—how coherent, logical, and grammatical the writing is—and the mechanical aspects of writing, such as spelling or handwriting. To write well takes time—time for planning, composing, and revising—and it is therefore difficult to assess in a short time. One option is to ask the individual to bring in a sample of his or her writing; however, in this situation we have no control over where and when the writing was done. Some tests measure writing skills by having the person write a sentence or several paragraphs about a picture. Sometimes these tests are timed to see how quickly the person can write. We can measure the quality of the composition, the number of words produced, the number of words spelled correctly, and the quality of the handwriting. This technique gives some indication of a person's writing skills.

To measure the mechanical skills involved in handwriting, there are tests that require copying shapes. We can compare a child's ability to copy to the ability of other children of the same age.

Testing for Mathematics Skills

A test of computational arithmetic skills should be administered to determine what the individual knows about the fundamental arithmetic operations of addition, subtraction, multiplication, and division. Consider the following subtraction error:

$$
\begin{array}{r}
43 \\
-\,27 \\
\hline
24
\end{array}
$$

The child has misunderstood the procedure and taken 3 away from 7 rather than 7 away from 3 (really 13). This child appears not to understand what subtraction means and also has trouble with place value—that is, understanding the columns for tens and ones.

Problem-solving is another mathematical skill that should be tested. For example, the following problem tests computational skills and reading and memory skills: Jason has $2.50 more than Jennifer and Jennifer has $1.30 more than Brad. If Jason has $7.30, how much money do Jennifer and Brad each have?

Solving the Assessment Crisis

An assessment crisis exists in the schools. Tragically, students who are struggling with learning disabilities cannot get help without formal testing. University and college students cannot get accommodations without this testing. And beyond school, individuals with learning disabilities who need accommodations for job qualification testing (e.g., the licensing examination to be a plumber) cannot get them without this testing. Often, students must wait eighteen months or even two years for an assessment. They will not get any extra help for their learning problems until they have a formal assessment. Of course, they or their parents can pay from $1,500 to $2,500 for a private assessment, but this cost is prohibitive for many families.

The assessments that I have described can be conducted by school personnel (for example, classroom teachers, special education teachers, reading specialists, learning assistants, and speech therapists) and take about thirty to forty-five minutes of individual testing and thirty-five to forty-five minutes of group testing. For the group testing, an entire class can be tested at one time. Organizations designed to help people with learning disabilities, for example, the International Dyslexia Association or the Learning Disabilities Association, can help parents demand this type of testing for their children or help students in universities and colleges demand it for themselves. A research project at a local university can sometimes provide this assessment at little or no cost. Unions and professional organizations may be able to provide help for their members who require accommodations for learning disabilities.

The real solution is for schools, school districts, post-secondary institutions, and ministries of education and other government bodies to accept achievement testing as the appropriate assessment to determine the absence or presence of a learning disability. This assessment should be provided free to all individuals. One could argue that this approach would be very expensive. It would cost approximately $150 per person, including test materials and time for testing and scoring. This cost is less than one-tenth the cost of a formal assessment and yields as much information. The costs to society of not identifying and treating learning disabilities are enormous. They are measured in terms of people having emotional problems, attempting suicide, spending time in prison, and failing to be part of the trained labour force that contributes to the economy of a country.

12

IQ Worship
Into the Quicksand

At age eight, Larry received a score of 78 on an IQ (intelligence quotient) test.[1] IQ scores have a mean of 100. Most people (68 per cent of people) score between 85 and 115. A score below 70 (2.3 per cent of people) is considered the intellectually handicapped range. Larry's score is in approximately the bottom 10 per cent of people. In the early 1980s, he was placed in a class for mentally retarded children and remained in such classes until age fourteen. I tested him when he was thirty-four and enrolled in a graduate program at a major Canadian university, having completed a BA in psychology with an A average.

Larry had great difficulty learning to read, spell, write, and do arithmetic calculations. When tested at age thirty-four, his IQ score was 119, well above average and better than about 85 per cent of the population; however, he still had significant problems with reading and spelling. He had difficulty with short-term memory tasks and had occasional difficulty with verb tenses and finding the right word when speaking. Larry displayed a profile of a dyslexic individual, yet at age eight he was called mentally retarded. He was fortunate enough to have a very determined personality and very supportive parents who fought for his right to be educated. Larry's supportive environment did not prevent or cure his reading disability; his reading problem remained throughout his schooling and into adulthood. However, his environment probably prevented Larry from developing the serious social problems that are often a consequence of an undetected and untreated learning disability. For many children with learning problems, the future does not include university or graduate school but jail, alcohol and drug abuse, and/or suicide.

The case described above is a very dramatic example of the consequences of using an IQ test score as part of diagnosing a reading disability. Almost everywhere in North America and in most developed countries, people who are suspected of having a learning disability are given IQ tests. Today a child with poor reading skills and an IQ of 78 would be labelled "developmentally delayed," "intellectually handicapped," or a "slow learner." The child might be said to have a "general learning disability," but it is unlikely that he or she would be labelled "reading disabled" or "dyslexic." Therefore this child would not receive intensive help with reading because it would be argued, incorrectly, that we should not expect better reading from an individual with this IQ level.

IQ Testing and the Myth of Intelligence

In the early 1960s when the concept of learning disabilities was first developed, it was considered important to show that people who were struggling with reading or mathematics were intelligent enough to learn to read or do mathematics. To determine whether they were capable of learning, they received an IQ test. They had to score above a certain level to receive help with learning disabilities, although the required level varied from place to place.

People generally assume that an IQ test measures intelligence, but there is no absolute standard of intelligence. Some people are good at mechanical skills and can fix a broken car, others can draw well, and some can define obscure words. Which is the real intelligence? Intelligence is an artificial construct, a product of the imagination of the test constructors. Some psychologists, such as Howard Gardner, insist that we should think about intelligence not as a single construct but composed of many different skills.[2]

For the most part, IQ tests measure what a child has learned, not what he or she is capable of learning in the future. They measure a particular kind of intelligence and compare one person's level to that of other people. They test a limited number of skills, including memory for numbers, mental arithmetic, fine motor coordination, factual knowledge of geography and history, and the ability to define words. If you give the correct definition of the words on the test, you are considered more intelligent than someone who does not know as many of the tested words. But it could also mean that you do not know the particular words on the test, and if other words had been tested you would have magically been "more intelligent." Intelligence tests also measure how well a person remembers letters and numbers after a brief time. This procedure actually measures memory; if you have a poor memory, are you really less intelligent? The IQ test measures whether or not you can solve arithmetic problems in your head without pencil and paper. If you need a pencil and paper to solve the problems, are you less intelligent? IQ tests do not measure reasoning or problem-solving skills or critical thinking, all of which are important aspects of intelligence.

What counts as intelligence is also influenced by culture. In the 1960s, what became known as the Chitling IQ test was introduced.[3] Test yourself on these questions:

> Cheap chitlings (not the kind you purchase at a frozen food counter) will taste rubbery unless they are cooked long enough. How soon can you quit cooking them to eat and enjoy them?
> (a) 45 minutes, (b) 2 hours, (c) 24 hours, (d) 1 week (on a low flame), (e) 1 hour.

> Many people say that "Juneteenth" (June 19) should be made a legal holiday because this was the day when:
> (a) the slaves were freed in the USA, (b) the slaves were freed in Texas, (c) the slaves were freed in Jamaica, (d) the slaves were freed in California, (e) Martin Luther King was born, (f) Booker T. Washington died.

> Which word is most out of place here?
> (a) splib, (b) blood, (c) gray, (d) spook, (e) black.

The correct answer to all of the above examples is (c). Imagine if these questions were part of the IQ test today. How would you score?

The IQ score is supposed to measure "potential," meaning that it is assumed to predict what a person is capable of. Yet educational institutions often specify that if an IQ test score is more than three years old, it is not valid and the person must be retested. This is the ultimate absurdity. If the IQ score were a true indicator of potential, why would it change?

I argue that IQ test scores are not useful in identifying learning disorders. Using IQ tests with children with learning disabilities creates a logical paradox. Most of these children have deficiencies in one or more of the component skills that are part of IQ tests—memory and/or language and/or fine motor skills. Therefore, their scores on IQ tests will underestimate their competence.[4] To then say that children with learning disabilities are less intelligent because they have these problems is illogical.

Because IQ scores are assumed to predict and set limits on academic performance, a child with a low IQ score is not expected to develop academic skills. In other words, we assume that the IQ score indicates how much reading, arithmetic, and so on a child can be expected to do. However, some children who have low scores on IQ tests—that is, scores less than 90 or even 80—have average or even above-average scores on reading tests.

In the 1980s, IQ scores became a mythical deity worshipped by learning disability professionals. In the ultimate expression of this worship, IQ became incorporated into a simple and seemingly elegant mathematical equation; according to this equation, a learning disability occurs when the IQ score is much higher than the reading (or arithmetic) score. The difference between IQ scores and reading scores led to what is called the "discrepancy definition of a learning disability." It became the basic criterion for identifying a learning disability.

The discrepancy score appears mathematical and scientific, but it can result in many children being misdiagnosed. For example, in some provinces, states, and countries, if a child is a poor reader but has no discrepancy between his or her IQ score and reading score, the child is not considered reading disabled.[5] That child is labelled "low achieving" and does not receive help for his or her problems with reading, writing, spelling, or arithmetic. Do children who have higher scores on an IQ test have a greater right to help for their problems with reading or mathematics than children with similar problems but lower IQ? This false assumption landed learning disability professionals in the quicksand, and we are still paying a very high price for it.

IQ Is Irrelevant to Learning Disabilities

To test the underlying assumptions of the discrepancy definition, I studied and compared data on two groups of children who had low reading scores.[6] One group had reading scores that were significantly lower than their IQ scores—children who would traditionally be called dyslexic—while the other group had low reading scores but these scores were not significantly lower than their IQ scores. These children were labelled poor readers. On a variety of reading and spelling tests, I found that there were *no differences* between these two groups. The children traditionally called learning disabled and those called poor readers performed similarly when tested for reading, spelling, and phonological processing in short-term memory. I found the same results in a study with adults who had reading disabilities.[7] Children with dyslexia (as defined by the discrepancy definition) made the same kind of reading errors as the children with lower IQ scores.[8] These findings suggest that a discrepancy between IQ scores and reading scores is not relevant in identifying who has learning disabilities. Therefore there is no need to use IQ tests to determine who has a learning disability. We need only use achievement tests.

The discrepancy definition leads to a ludicrous situation. People with high IQ scores and average reading scores (or in some cases above average reading scores) are called dyslexic—just because of the difference between their scores—when they do not have a reading problem.

There is also other evidence that shows that the concept of intelligence is unnecessary in diagnosing reading disabilities. One study I conducted divided children with reading disabilities into groups based on their IQ level. I compared these groups on a variety of reading and spelling tasks, and in spite of wide differences in their IQ levels, there were no differences between the groups on these reading tasks. Since the groups were quite similar in relation to reading-related performance, administering an IQ test would not provide useful information about how to help the children with their reading problems. Even on a reading comprehension test, a higher IQ was not sufficient to compensate for a reading disability.[9]

If IQ scores really determined the level of reading capability, this result should not have occurred. It did occur because IQ scores do not predict the ability to benefit from remediation. Children of different IQ levels are equally likely to benefit from remedial programs.[10] This research result is especially important because it means that we should help all children who are having reading problems, whatever their IQ scores.

Very recent research on brain imaging has found no differences in brain functioning between children who are dyslexic and have high IQ scores and children who are dyslexic and have lower IQ scores.[11]

David and Goliath and the IQ Score

David was a child from a minority background who lived in the state of Michigan. His parents were blue-collar workers who did not have much money. David had an IQ score of 81 (technically called low average, but still in the average range), but there was no discrepancy between his low score on a reading test and his IQ. Therefore, the administrators of the school system where he was enrolled refused to give him help for his reading problems. Like the biblical hero who bore the same name, David and his parents battled the system. It was a long and difficult struggle, and one stone (a letter of protest) was not sufficient to win the fight; a lengthy court battle followed. David finally slew the Goliath of the system, but it was a bitter and expensive fight. The thousands of dollars spent on lawyers' fees and salaries for court officers could have been used to provide remedial help for David's dyslexia.

Out of the Quicksand?

After hitting bottom with IQ testing, we began the climb upward. Today some provinces in Canada do not require IQ testing for a diagnosis of a learning disability, but others do. Where this requirement exists, it means that help for the child or accommodations for the adult in a college or university will be delayed or sometimes denied.[12] In a recent call for research, the US government acknowledged that we do not need the discrepancy definition. However, in many official definitions of a learning disability the discrepancy definition is still used. Unfortunately, still today people with reading or mathematics difficulties and with lower IQ scores often do not get help, even if their IQ scores are not very low.

The following conversation reflects how the IQ test is still an issue today for people with learning disabilities. Names have been changed to protect the innocent and the guilty.

Jane Lowe, the coordinator of a centre intended to help students with learning disabilities at a large Canadian university, asserted, "I will not accept your diagnosis of dyslexia for Joanne Ridgely because you did not do the IQ test."

"Why do you want the IQ test?" I asked.

"Because I want the IQ test," she responded.

I explained that Joanne had graduated from high school with a B– average and A grades in mathematics and chemistry and physics, and that she was clearly capable of university-level work.

The coordinator insisted, "I want the IQ test. I will not give her any accommodations or help her unless we have an IQ score."

Me: Why?

J. L.: Because we want the IQ test.

Me: Is there a minimum IQ that is required?

J. L.: No.

Me: Why do you want the IQ test?

J. L.: Because we want the IQ test.

Me: Do you require a discrepancy between her IQ score and her reading score to prove that she has dyslexia?

J. L.: No.

Me: What information will you get from the IQ test?

J. L.: We want to have the IQ test score.

This conversation sounds like an excerpt from *Catch-22* or a Monty Python skit, but unfortunately it is real.

13

Abuses of the IQ Test
The Case of Johnny

Johnny wrote to me, "The way I feel, even if one child is misdiagnose by an IQ test and labeled as a moron for life, the school system should be made libel."[1] Johnny, a retired physical education teacher from New York City, shared his story with me when he was seventy-seven years old. In telling Johnny's story, mostly in his own words, I have chosen not to correct any errors. Johnny's words clearly express his feelings, although his spelling, grammar, and choice of words may sometimes be incorrect (which is a pattern that is characteristic of dyslexia). We need to look below the surface mistakes and pay attention to the ideas. Johnny shows great insight into the futility of using IQ tests to categorize or define children's abilities.

His writing shows that problems with spelling and grammar should not blind us to the real value of the words of people with dyslexia. Of course, schools need to teach spelling, grammar, and vocabulary, as well as composition, but even the best teaching may fail in the case of a dyslexic person.

Johnny's Early School Years

Johnny was the son of poor Italian immigrant parents in New York City. The name on his birth certificate was Giovanni, but everyone called him by his American name, Johnny. For the first few years of school, Johnny was popular with his classmates and a very good punch ball player. A pretty girl named Jane was his secret love.

"During lunch hour we would play punch ball in the school yard and there were always a lot of children watching the game. When it was my turn to get up, I'd kind of look of to the side very sullenly and watch Jane cheer me on. As I proceeded to punch the ball out of my hand I'd whisper to myself, this is for you Jane and the ball would explode out of my hand for a home run. I remember a classmate coming over to me and saying the word is out that Jane likes you."

It was the early 1940s and Johnny was in a regular fifth grade class. Being dyslexic, Johnny struggled with reading, writing, and spelling. However, learning disabilities were not recognized then. His teacher frequently yelled at him and belittled him in front of the class. He could not get any support from his parents: "There was no complaining to my father, he would have beat me. We were poor. My father was just a milkman making ends meet. The teachers were always right. Emmigrants from Italy, they were grateful to be here."

The school decided to give Johnny an IQ test. He struggled with understanding words and expressing himself and remembering words and numbers, all characteristic of dyslexia. An IQ test measures these abilities. His score was 67, in the range that today we would call intellectual disability or intellectual handicap.

The school did not explore the reasons for his low score. There was no understanding of dyslexia and how that could influence the score on an IQ test. A child's family background can also play a role in his or her score. Johnny's parents did not have any books in the house (except the Bible) and could barely read. They were uneducated and were forced to leave school in their small village in Italy when they were young to help their parents on the farm. They did not finish the fourth grade. Did the school even consider these factors? Of course not.

"One day a student monitor from the retarded class approached Miss Jones and ask for me. He was to escort me to a room for psychological testing. There was a desk placed in front of that room reserved for the physically mature monitor so no one could enter room while I was being tested. I will never forget his words, 'Hey man, if you fail this test your going to the retarded class for dummies.'

"Nobody had to tell me about dummys. My sister and brother were in this class since the first grade. They were two years older than me. I myself was embarrassed for them when I saw them parading threw the hall with there class or at the assembly. They were an atypical bunch of students and witness the looks of condescension by other students.

"Now I was going to take a test that would condemn me if I failed. You talk about being nervous I was shaking. No wonder I did poorly. Mrs. Jones would have done anything to get me out of her class she hated me. Those are harsh words but I know what teachers are cabable [this is an example of the type of errors that people with dyslexia make that may indicate subtle problems with speech perception] doing, I was one for 35 years for the same system. My point is conditions are very important when taking an examination. . . . I remember the young femal psychologist being very pleasant to calm me down but it did not work my nervousness took over and encountered many nervous blocks."

Imagine this young boy, smart enough to recognize the importance of the testing. If he "failed," he would be put in the "dummy class." He was so frightened that he trembled as he answered the questions. Often his mind went blank. How tragic that a system does this to young people.

Not surprisingly, he obtained a low score on the IQ test. There are several possible reasons for this: perhaps because of the language requirements of the test; perhaps because he was nervous; perhaps because the IQ test measures memory, vocabulary, and ability to express yourself, which are all problems for many people with dyslexia.

Condemned

"I sat in the front desk to the right of Mrs. Jones' desk in full view of the attendance chart inserted in an envelope placed on the side of the desk. Ever morning an attendance monitor picks it up and replaces it with a new one. I noticed that on the new attendance sheet there was a red slip of paper attach to it with my name on it. I then leaned forward to get a better view. It read, 'Johnny Salerno transferred from 5B to the ungraded class.' A few hours later the ungraded class teacher, Mrs. Casey, knocks on the classroom door and is met by Mrs. Baker. Mrs. Baker points towards me and wispers 'that's the boy.' Mrs. Casey, a tall eldery women with a black dress approaches me with a big smile. She says come with me Johnny. I sit at my desk in disbelief and don't move. It was a scene from a James Cagney movie, *Angels with Dirty Faces*, when he doesn't want go to the electric chair. She literaly drags me through the hall. I was on the linoleum floor I remember being dragged down the hall balling like a baby.

"When finally got control of myself, she escorted me into my new class. It was strange. There were tables instead of desks and shop tables to the rear of room. Mrs. Casey would speak to us with such kindness as if we were mental cases. Oh how in the world did this ever happen to me.

"Being in this class I developed an inferior complex, It manifested itself in different ways. The normal kids were carrying books. I never had homework, I never carried books. I could never engage in a conversation with a pretty girl. I was made to believe I was different."

We can still hear the pain in his voice sixty-seven years later.

"My poor sister (Angela) and brother (Tommy) were put into a retarded class in the 1st grade. Every time I think about it I get furious. Believe me, they had potential. They are both living and are 79 years old. Both have very little self-esteem and self-confidence. What an injustice, exploiting ignorant immigrants!

"Tommy and Angela spent their entire school experience in the opportunity class (another name for class for retarded students) only to graduate from junior high school at 16 years old with a fourth grade reading score. Watching my sister and brother survive over the years has been a shameful experience. My pop and mom never went to school for any reason to inquire as to how we were doing. Pop was a milkman, also navy yard worker during the war. He was a terrific billiard player and made money shooting pool and a real male chauvinist who slapped my mother around on many occasions. My mother spoke broken English, had a great singing voice, never went to work, loved and took care of her children. Pop was grateful to be an American, and he trusted the system. They would never think of going to school to make sure the children where doing well or to be advocates for their children."

Life changed for Johnny after he entered the "retarded class." The stigma was enormous. His friends ignored him (they did not want to be with the "dummies") and Jane lost interest in him. "You couldn't blame them if you saw the make up of the class, parading down the hall as one group and into auditorium in full view of the students. We looked like freaks. I was heart broken and embarrassed." Johnny thought that the parents of the other children told their children not to associate with the "dummy kids," and he was probably right.

"I'll never forget this one summer day. I'm 11 or 12 years old on my way home from school. I see Jane from a distance holding hands with a boy walking towards her house. A surge of jealously overcame me. I followed them to Jane's house. I snuck be hide a truck. In full view I saw the boy escort her up the stairs open the door to the vestibule and close it. The doors were made of wood and panel glass so I was able to see what they were doing. He took her in his arms and kissed her. Again, I got jealous and depressed, and said to myself, it could have been me if it weren't for that ungraded class."

Johnny recounted some of his experiences in that class. "One of my teachers was Mrs. O Neill. Her face resembled W. C. Fields and she was nervous and extremely insecure. If the class was noisy and she was not able to control it, she would run over to the door and peek through the hole to see if the principal was coming." To control the class she brought in cheap jewellery and little toys to bribe the class to be quiet, "anything to bribe us to keep us quiet. How pathetic.

"The class consisted of a range of children from 11 to 15 years old. She would put us into groups develop our reading skills. It just didn't work, no discipline. Even though I did extremely well in all my subjects there was not enough individual tutoring to bring me up to my grade level. Their was no incentive to main-stream me into the normal grades. Nobody cared there hands were tided we were sentence to a life of the uneducable. It was futile. Even if you shouted out a loud 'Give me another chance in the grades I know I can do it.' IQ was a legal means to screen you in these classes and no teacher was willing to stick there neck out for you. . . . I began to loose confidence and succumb to there ways. The months were passing by and I was falling behind in all academic subjects."

Attempting to Gain Acceptance

Johnny described his "inner rage that was not permitted to come out. . . . My mother was a worrier and could not handle trouble and because I loved her I tried my best to keep out of trouble. I took my frustrations out in sports." And in fighting. "It didn't matter how big the individual was I would never back down I would never back down. Man, I would have done anything for love and acceptance."

One day when Johnny was bullied by a boy who was much older than he was, they fought outside the school grounds. "My body was like a coil, stalking him like an animal. What an opportunity to let off some rage. I remember him striking me with the first blow, It really did not bother me. The thought was this is for real he is trying to hurt me. The crowd was in a frenzy. I saw my chance to hit him and I did placing my right fist on to his jaw. I had knock him out cold. I was frighten. I thought I might have killed him. Finally a teacher came and broke the crowd up and carried the bully to the nurse's office. He recovered. I was called to the office about the incident; they gave me some warnings and it was left at that. No parents were involved."

Like Johnny, children with learning disabilities often feel that they have to prove themselves. They are doing poorly in school, so they have to be the leaders and even the fighters in the schoolyard and will do anything to achieve the respect and admiration of their peers. But Johnny also found a creative way to get the attention he craved. He suggested to his teacher that their class participate in the school's weekly assembly program.

"It was during second world war and I came up with this idea with me being an army sergeant. I would line my class and rehearse a series of marching steps to the ryhum of panio music and me yelling out cadence. What do you do in the infanry? The class would respond You March You March You March! What do you do when your back is packed, You March You March You March! The Hard Way, The Hard Way etc. Then we sang Bless them all bless them all, the long the short and the tall. Well I don't have to tell you how we were recieved the applause was esstounding. Those kids and myself felt loved and belonged, accepted by our peers."

Escape

Johnny assumed that he would stay in the ungraded class forever and grew increasingly unhappy. However, an accident of fate and some clever actions on his part changed his life. He wrote, "I've been very lucky," but I think that it was more than luck. Johnny had the sort of intelligence that no IQ test measures.

On a hot summer day he was playing in front of his house, when an old woman dressed in black and with rosary beads in her hand came along and asked him questions about religion. Johnny recounts the conversation:

"Are you Catholic? Do you go to church? Did you make your communion? Does your mother and father go to church? I said I was Catholic, but all the other questions were no. She was genuinely upset. Your going to hell If you don't make your communion and go to church, is your mother home I want to speak to her. She did go up to speak with her. It turns out, we had to go to mass every Sunday and we must go to religious instruction every Wednesday at 2PM. That meant we were permitted by the Board of Ed to leave one hour earlier. I was eleven and I welcomed the challenge to memorize all these prayers. . . . Going to church introduce me to confession and thats when I got my break in life. I was lucky!

"At St. Mary's church during confession I told the preist [Father O'Sullivan] all my sins, such as disobeying my mother, entertaining bad thoughts, and missing mass." The priest asked him whether there were any other problems. "At that very moment, some how I un-nerved myself to explained to him my unhappiness with being in a ungraded class. He did not have the slightest idea as to what I was talking about." The priest sensed Johnny's strong emotions and invited Johnny to see him that evening at the rectory at six p.m.

That night Johnny was extremely nervous when he went to the old rectory next to the church. "The old rectory was next to the church. I walked up the concrete stairs took a deep breath and rang the door bell, nobody came. I was so nervous, I was about to leave when I heard foot steps coming down from a squeaky staircase. The door opened a elderly women the maid said, 'Can I help you?' I said, My name is Johnny and Father O'Sullivan would like to see me. Oh yes he is expecting you, please wait in the reception room. The house reeked with the odor of Irish stew. Suddenly I heard footsteps coming down the squeaky steps." Father O'Sullivan entered dressed in his long black cassock and introduced himself. "So tell me about this ungraded class," he said. Johnny gathered his courage and told the priest his story.

"Father, I have been in this special class for almost four years and I feel I am a lot smarter than any one of those kids but they wont take me out and put me in a regular class. Father, when I went as far as the fifth grade I was never left back before I went into the CRMD class. What's a CRMD class Father asked. Children with retarded mental development I replied. . . . Father O'Sullivan understood my hurt; he indeed was a compassioned man.

"He knew I wanted another chance. I told him the class was composed of different children ages ranging from thirdteen to sixteen with different levels of intelligence. . . . I told him that my teacher Mrs. O Neill reconized that I was smarter than most of the kids she explained their was nothing she could do. Once your in, your in, never mainstreamed. No teacher was willing to take on that responsibility. We are talking about NYC Board Of Education. Father O'Sullivan asked me the name of the school. He said he would look into it and I left."

Three or four days later Johnny's teacher, Mrs. Casey, received a note and told Johnny to report to the principal's office. "When I arrived at the office, the principal Mr. Jefferson hands me some papers and says 'you are being transferred from this school to St. Mary's Parochial School and you are to report tomorrow.' It was hard to believe I felt I just had been released from prison. I don't remember my mother or father given consent. I guess Father O'Sullivan just took the bull by the horns and did it."

How ironic! Johnny used his intelligence to get out of the retarded class and yet his score on the IQ test was quite low.

"No-way was I ever going to embarrass Father O'Sullivan for sticking his neck out for me. I was determine to do well whatever the cost what ever means necessary. I was now going to carry books, do homework be like everbody else. Let us understand I'm doing this all by myself, no help from my brothers, sister, mother, or father.

"I was about fourteen years old just being to shave under my neck. I was big and husky for my age, very agile and a good athlete. I was put in the fifth grade. It was embarrassing but I was determine to stick it out. I behaved like an angle and develop a humble quality. No way was I going to get sidetracked. I waited to long to be a part of, to hold a book, to study with a purpose. I was big, so many of the kids took a shine to me. I remember having trouble with the subject religion. A student, John, offered to help me. He was half the size of me and a very smart boy. He told his mother about me and she said it was alright for me come over the house and have study sessions. That I did. The principal and father O'Sullivan saw that I was progressing quickly. They skipped me from 5 to 6 and 7 to 8. When I took the city wide Regents [statewide examinations in each subject at the end of each school year] I scored 90. My partial pay back was I learned Latin and became an altar boy.

"The effects of my four years in the ungraded class lowered my self esteem, my confidence, and accelerated my inferiority complex. In my adult life it manifests itself in different ways. Once you got in this class you never got out. Where was the modivation to get back into the regular grades?

"During this time filtering system was not to good. It was a dumping ground. Why couldn't they put us in a separate school and spare us the humiliation of walking through halls as a group, with students gaping at us as though we were a freak show."

At Work and in the Air Force

Johnny's father encouraged him to learn a trade. Being a plumber, an electrician, or a bricklayer provided security, so Johnny attended a vocational high school. "My major was avaition. I did well, Vice President of the school my senior year,

Played four years of varsity baseball and was captain my senor year. I won the oratorical contest a few years straight."

Every summer Johnny worked as a dishwasher or busboy, and when he graduated he worked at various odd jobs. "No one in my area went to college. It was unheard of; to become a fireman, a cop was the ultimate. My neighborhood was very much into sports. I excelled in baseball and got a contract to play professional baseball with the cubs farm system at nineteen. I played for the Hickory Rebels in North Carolina. When the season was over I got a job working for the city as a provisional playground director for the city."

Johnny's work was interrupted when he was drafted during the Korean War. He chose to join the air force. "I became a medic in the service and served two years in Alaska and to years In Sacramento, California. At Mather AFB, I was in special services because of my special ability as a baseball player and my ability to organize activities. Here I rubbed shoulders and made great friends. Many were college graduates and they encourage me to continue my education. I had this feeling that I am not worthy of college. It's for some one else, not this Italian guy from Brooklyn.

"I did take some college courses in the evening at Sacramento junior college to find out if I could handle it. I could, fighting these negitive feelings. I was a few months away from being discharged. The goverment offered us guys in the military two months early out If you enroll in a creited college. I was entitled to the GI BILL. Prior to being discharged from the service, I enrolled at Pasadena City College. No problem getting in. They excepted my high school diploma and six credits from evening college. I carried 16 credits and ready for this new adventure. It was a casual school. Students walking around with flip flops, shorts, Hawaiian shirts. I thought to myself hey! I can get use to this. I did not feel out of place because there were other GIs. My tuition was paid buy goverment and took a job as a dancing instructor with Arthur Murry dancing studio to supplement my income."

Johnny recalled meeting the noted author Frank McCourt, who also came from a poor background. They discovered that they had both fought in the Korean War and, as a result, were able to get funding to go to university, which would have been impossible without it. Many young people enter the military at least in part for the promise of funding for their education. Perhaps we should spend some of the money that we spend on fighting wars and give scholarships for higher education to students who cannot afford it.

After one semester Johnny went home to Brooklyn and lived with his parents again. He got back his previous job as a playground director but then was laid off because by then the city required two years of college for that job. Johnny had to work, so he took a janitor's job at the same playground until he could figure out his next move. Through a conversation with an elderly veteran, he learned that he qualified for disability benefits because he had injured his back and knee while playing baseball for the air force team and was hospitalized for a time during his service.

"Recieving disability meant I would get tuition fully paid by the government, plus books and a subsistence [allowance]. I knew I was not a bright guy. I needed a lot time to study and catch up. The problem was would they except me in NUY. I took the entrance examine and they felt I was a boarder line case. After all I was a vocational high school graduate, it was not academic. They suggested I speak to the chairman of the physical education

department. If she excepted me they would enroll me uncon-
ditionally. If I passed all my coarses the first year then they would
matriculate me.

"My first year at NUY was tough. It was a weeding out period.
I never had cemistry in high school and I did poorly in writing."
Johnny found a solution. "A classmate, Steve, was a poor dancer
but knew his cemistry. He was getting married and did not know
how to do the waltz. The deal was you teach me cemistry I teach
you to waltz, he went for it. I got a C+ in chemistry."

Johnny almost failed English literature, but his professor
gave him a chance to revise his compositions. "I worked hard on
those compositions with some help from my brother Freddie. I
managed to get a C. I remember getting a B− average for the
year and it was enough to matriculate. The rest was quite easy, I
graduated with a B+ average. Got a BA in Health and Physical
Education." Johnny became a teacher and taught physical education in the New York City schools for many years.

Finding Himself, but with Lasting Scars

During his teaching years and in retirement, Johnny became
very interested in acting. "I learned to deal with my nerviousness,
memorize lines, communicate, and express emotions that I dare
not express in real life. I accepted failure as a means to learn from
it, to cope with rejection. The socialazation factor was fabulous.
I was doing some thing for me after giving so much of myself to
[school] children."

Although he was a good actor, Johnny could not shake the
insecurities he had developed during his student years in the
ungraded class. He could not afford to see a psychologist, so he
decided that teaching was more secure than acting. Nevertheless,

he stayed involved in acting for over thirty years because he found emotional strength and self-esteem from acting, and he made friends with other actors.

Johnny will never get over the resentment and the trauma of being put in the class for "retarded children." "All these years I have endoured this feeling of being cheated." Although he had a long and eventually satisfying career, a good marriage, a child and grandchild, and financial security, the scars are still with him.

Johnny's Dream

Johnny recounted a dream. He is in a courtroom talking to a judge.

"My brother and sister are sitting behind a table, they are twins, and they both were put in a retarded class at six years old. They are now both 79 years old, both have a fifth grade reading level and both are on welfare. It is my opinion the Board of Ed. made a gross mistake. What means of measurement did they have for intelligence in 1937, for a child of six? or did they subconsciously inherit Hitler's philosophy. [Hitler institutionalized and killed intellectually handicapped children.] I often think about my brother and sister, the bum deal they got being put in a ungraded class so young. Taking an IQ test is like taking blood pressure. The scores go up and down."

Johnny's view of the CRMD classes has not changed over the years. He wrote, "When I think of the CRMD classes and its philosophy what a crock of manuer. It was set up to give individual attention so the child can catch up. Bull. There are 18 to 20 children different levels of intelligence, different ages, what a con. Sometimes the teacher would hold them in groups but it never worked. I was hungry for information but I had to wait my turn. These classes were holding areas to keep them from the main stream. Contain them, give them busy work. Hold them until there 16 then give them a special graduation."

In his dream, Johnny says, "These actions should be held accountable. So I am asking the courts, to recognize that the New York City School System made a mistake and be accountable for that mistake in monitory means.

"The judge looks at me and says, 'congratulations you did well.'"

I wish that Johnny's dream would come true. It is too late for his brother and sister and too late to erase Johnny's pain.

Lessons Learned about IQ Testing

Johnny correctly doubts the validity of IQ testing. "When I retired from teaching I decided to take a IQ test with the VA [Veterans Affairs]. It was for vocational rehabilitation. I scored very high. There are so many circumstances that play into the conduciveness of a healthy testing situation."

What have we learned from Johnny's story? We need to identify children with dyslexia early in their schooling and help them, not abandon them in classes where it is assumed that they are too stupid to learn. Johnny can tell a good story with vivid and colourful language. His ideas are excellent, but his spelling and grammar mistakes are typical of what you find with dyslexia. He sometimes omits letters, confuses homophones such as *by* and *buy* and *their* and *there*, and uses wrong verb tenses. You can hear echoes of his New York accent when he drops the *r*'s or writes *d* instead of *t*. But his message comes through with emotion.

The misdiagnosis that happened with Johnny still occurs today in more subtle ways. For example, IQ tests are given inappropriately to children who have English as a second language, children from homes in which there are limited opportunities for language development, and to people who have good visual-spatial skills but very poor verbal skills. In many states and provinces in North America, there must be a discrepancy between children's IQ scores and their reading scores for them to be designated as learning disabled. Still today the system is a quicksand of bureaucracy and has long waiting lists for testing. People with learning disabilities who want to enter post-secondary education in the United States and Canada are often required to pay privately for IQ and other tests that cost as much as $2,500.

Johnny poignantly asked me if he would have been dyslexic if he had been born into a different family but with the same brain. The answer is yes, but his experiences might have been quite different. If his parents had been in a position to advocate for him with the school and to ensure that he received the special help that he needed, and if his talents in sports and acting had been recognized, he could have developed self-confidence. Perhaps he might have become a successful actor. Instead, he felt inferior and spent years hidden away in a class for "the retarded."

My dream is that what happened to Johnny will not happen to any other child and that we will recognize and treat all learning problems before they lead to negative emotional and social consequences.

14

Not Stupid
A Tale of Two Teachers

If I were to make up cases to illustrate learning problems, it would be hard to invent better examples than those of two teachers who have written thoughtful and poignant accounts of their struggles in school. One is a teacher who could not learn to read; the other is a teacher who could not spell, do mathematics, or write compositions. These two teachers are textbook examples of the two most common types of learning disabilities: dyslexia, and written-output and mathematics disability.

The Teacher Who Couldn't Read

A teacher who could not read? Impossible, I thought, until I read John Corcoran's memoir, *The Teacher Who Couldn't Read*. John creatively taught secondary school for seventeen years, hiding his inability to read. Numerous former students say he was the best teacher they ever had.

At the age of fifty-seven, John Corcoran revealed his startling story to the world. He was clearly dyslexic, but the educational system never recognized his disability. He struggled with reading in school. He was terrified when he had to read out loud. He could not even recite the alphabet or sing the alphabet song. He had trouble hearing sounds and relating them to letters. When he was asked to say the alphabet in second grade, he says that he wanted to shrink and hide in the inkwell (school desks used to have inkwells). He only learned to read at age forty-eight.

The Buzzards

John was placed in the "dumb" class (his label) in second grade and the Buzzards reading group in fourth grade. He knew who the Buzzards were; they were the non-readers. (I suppose it would have been worse if they were called "the Vultures.") Assignments in the Buzzards group only reinforced John's idea that he was stupid. He knew that his reading difficulties were not caused by his eyesight because he could see the "remotest star" and also help his mother thread a needle.

John had many of the symptoms of dyslexia. He sometimes had difficulty hearing sounds in words, relating these sounds to letters, and pronouncing words. He said *liberry* instead of *library*, perhaps because he could not distinguish the *r* sound.

No one recognized or helped him with his reading problem. Teachers told his parents not to worry, that he would "catch up." He was ashamed of his inability to read. The words on the page mocked and embarrassed him. In his memoir, one can sense his bitterness about his school experience. He writes that teachers who do not make sure children learn how to read, write, and spell are cheating them.

John repeatedly suffered embarrassment at the hands of his teachers. He describes one who waited for him to read out loud and taunted him by saying sarcastically, "Cat got your tongue."

One teacher called him "immature" and "unmotivated." Another teacher hit him for not completing the sentences in his workbook and for "refusing" to read the material on the blackboard (he was not able to read it). Not only did the teacher hit him, but he also allowed other boys in the class to hit John. The beatings did not hurt him as much as the humiliation he experienced. He kept his pain and embarrassment bottled inside. He lived in fear that the mask would slip and his reading problem would be revealed to all.

When teachers discovered that he could not read and spell, they told him to "try harder." You are probably wondering, as I did while reading his autobiography, why he did not ask his teachers for help. John really believed that his reading problem was his fault; he was the guilty one. No one recognized the basis of his reading problem or helped him cope with it.

Nausea overwhelmed John on Fridays before spelling tests. He hated report card day and once ripped his report card to shreds. His school days were filled with fear, humiliation, and emotional trauma.

Later in life, his inability to read caused ongoing problems. Once he had to fill out a form to get a permit for some construction work that he was doing. He manipulated a former student (the clerk at the office where he got the form) to fill out the form. People with dyslexia quite commonly use manipulation to get others to do their work. We all dislike filling out forms, but those of us who are not dyslexic are able to do so even if we hate it. Dyslexics cannot. In restaurants John could not read menus, so he always ordered what someone else before him ordered.

Talents and Abilities

John's life was not, however, all tragedy and terror. Like most children with learning disabilities, he had some talents. He was athletic, was always chosen to be on sports teams, and was popular on the playground. He could show off his athletic prowess and his strength and speed at recess. He was the class clown and delighted in disrupting the class with antics and wisecracks.

John writes that even though he could not read books, he could "read" people. Many people with dyslexia have excellent social perception; that is, they understand facial expressions, gesture, and tone of voice quite well. John relates the story of when he recognized the lecherous intentions of a priest and protected his sisters by preventing them from being alone with the priest.

Coping as a Student

As I read John's account, I wondered how he completed high school and obtained a university degree without reading. His descriptions of his various tactics are both amazing and horrifying. He would laboriously copy homework from others. He was quite accustomed to asking others to do his homework or write papers for him. He used ingenious methods of cheating. A girlfriend helped him through college.

He became a cat burglar, climbing up buildings and breaking into offices to steal copies of tests. During a final exam, he once dropped the test booklet out a window and had a friend answer the questions and then return it to him.

When teachers discussed topics, John paid close attention and developed his listening and memory skills. To learn about a topic, he watched movies and TV programs and looked at the pictures in *National Geographic* magazine.

All of these machinations had a price. He lived in constant fear that his mask would fall off, revealing his inability to read.

Coping as a Teacher and a Parent

As a teacher, John created an oral and visual learning environment for his students. He had the students work in groups. He graded students by talking to them individually and grading their oral work. He had students grade each other's papers. He had one of his students call the roll.

He "read" books to his daughter by looking at the pictures and making up stories. It worked with familiar stories such as *Cinderella* and *Snow White and the Seven Dwarfs*. However, one day his daughter asked him to read to her a book in which he did not recognize the story from the pictures. He was trapped: he could not read the title. He quickly made up a story, but his daughter told him that was the wrong story. John's wife overheard the exchange from the next room and suddenly realized that John could not read.

Winning the War with Words

John eventually did learn to read. A literacy volunteer taught him the basics of reading. He received intensive instruction in the Lindamood-Bell method, which teaches people the relationship between letters and their sounds and how their mouth makes the sounds of the letters. This method helps people understand the differences between the sounds of different letters.

John Corcoran's story is one of turmoil and eventual triumph over his disability. He now works tirelessly to help other dyslexics. In 1997 he founded the John Corcoran Foundation, a non-profit organization dedicated to the eradication of illiteracy.

In 2008, he published a second book, *The Bridge to Literacy*, in which he proposes solutions for US illiteracy.

The Teacher Who Thought He Was a Dunce

Daniel Pennac, an award-winning writer from France, is a retired teacher of French language and literature. He wrote many acclaimed novels, books for children, illustrated books, and an autobiography, *Chagrin d'école*, translated into English as *School Blues*. Although he received bachelor's and master's degrees in French language and literature, as a student, he was, in his own words, a "dunce." He struggled with writing, spelling, and mathematics and clearly had a written-output and mathematics disability.

In addition to difficulty with spelling and mathematics, Daniel had difficulty remembering dates and places, and he seemed incapable of learning foreign languages. He claims that it took him one year to learn to write the letter *a*. He had to repeat his final year in school. He was not talented in music or sports.

Disorganization was one of Daniel's problems; he forgot his books and often did not do his homework. He was afraid to admit that he did not understand the homework assignments and made up excuses such as that the boiler exploded. He was quite creative with excuses: "I did not do my homework because I spent half the night in cyberspace defeating the soldiers of Evil, which, by the way, I exterminated down to the last one."[1]

Throughout his school career, he was at the bottom or next to the last in his class. Teachers called him lazy. He was not dyslexic; even as a child he loved reading and devoured books on history and philosophy. He read novels but not school books.

Daniel believed that everyone understood ideas and mathematics much more quickly than he did. He relates that he worked hard to find the common denominator of one fraction—an impossible task. He felt that even the dog was smarter than he was.

He thought that teachers were there to block his progress. Fear, worry, bitterness, humiliation, anger, and dissatisfaction all surged through his brain. He believed that his teachers and parents thought that he was purposefully trying to fail. He assumed that they were right, and concluded, "I am nothing." He had suicidal thoughts, a common problem among people with learning disabilities.

Daniel compensated for his learning disabilities by becoming the class clown and "chatterbox." Fond of practical jokes, he describes one incident where he tied kippers to the exhaust pipe of a teacher's car. The car reeked of kippers for days.

Daniel tried to understand his problem. He came from an intellectual middle-class family in which there were no drug or alcohol problems. He suspects that he would have resorted to joining a gang as an escape from the hell of school, but fortunately at the time there were no gangs in his neighbourhood.

He writes about the loneliness that he felt as the "dunce." He sought approval from adults. He compared himself with his more successful siblings. Even when he became a successful teacher, novelist, and TV personality, he was apprehensive about his success. In reading his autobiography, one has the feeling that he has never completely erased the feeling of being a dunce.

The Teacher Who Saved Daniel

After suffering for nine years in school, Daniel encountered a teacher who changed his life. This teacher recognized that Daniel was an ingenious storyteller who invented clever excuses for why he did not do his homework. He excused Daniel from doing essays and, instead, assigned him the task of writing a novel. Daniel was required to write one chapter each week. He could choose the topic, but *no* spelling mistakes were allowed.

His dictionary became worn and tattered. Thanks to this teaching strategy, Daniel learned to write, and eventually he earned bachelor's and master's degrees in French language and literature.

Teaching

Daniel argues persuasively that teachers must take responsibility for their students, even the ones who have trouble learning. His experiences in school gave him empathy for his students. He helped his students understand and memorize carefully chosen texts—beginning with short texts—to help develop their confidence. He refused to mark what he called absurd answers; his aim was to get the students to think. He taught them to play chess, which gave them a feeling of accomplishment. In one ingenious assignment, he asked his students to make up questions for the examination and answer them. Most of them did an excellent job and were able to demonstrate their knowledge.

He aptly describes the circle of blame for failing students: the universities blame the high schools, the high schools blame the elementary schools, the elementary schools blame the parents, and the parents blame the universities for their inadequate teacher education programs.

Lessons

The accounts written by John Corcoran and Daniel Pennac are filled with anxiety, fear, anger, and resentment, but they also tell of eventual success. From their stories, we can learn much about how to help students with learning disabilities. Still today, teacher education programs need to provide more instruction for teaching reading, spelling, writing, and mathematics to students with learning disabilities.

15

Not Lazy
The Case of Darryl

I am happy to have someone diagnose the problems
I have been experiencing all my life. There's something
reassuring when someone else can identify and verbalize
the difficult struggle I have been going through.

—Darryl, when he was first told that he was dyslexic

I met Darryl when he was thirty-five.[1] He had finished high school and completed a diploma in chemical technology at a local community college, but he read words and understood what he read at the level of a sixth grader. When he came across a new word, an unfamiliar term, or a long name, he had trouble sounding it out. His spelling was poor; he probably would not have passed a fifth-grade spelling test.

As a young boy in school, Darryl clearly had dyslexia, but the school system ignored his difficulties, failed to diagnose his reading problem, and did not provide the help that he needed. For thirty years, his parents, teachers, and psychologists ignored his problems or told him he was lazy or that his reading problems were "emotional." Darryl started kindergarten with a smiling face and a new white shirt and a blue bow tie. As he went through school, each year the school photos show the smile fading and a knitted brow becoming more pronounced.

Darryl saved all his report cards and graciously shared them with me in the hope that they would help parents, teachers, and others to understand what someone with a learning disability experiences.

Kindergarten and Grade 1

Darryl's difficulties began in kindergarten. He had difficulty with language and did not speak clearly. His vocabulary was limited compared to that of other children his age, and he struggled with learning to read. He had trouble learning to listen and follow instructions, and he was easily frustrated. His teacher wrote to his parents that "he will have to improve" and "next year he will have to put his mind to the fact that he will have to remember and retain some of the information that he hears." These problems are all signs of a child at risk for dyslexia. The teacher interpreted his difficulties as resulting from laziness. She did note that he was "cooperative, neat, has good fine motor control and an interest and talent in music." He was also called "a good little boy." These descriptions are hard to reconcile with the label "lazy."

It is a very common assumption that if children who are struggling with reading tried harder, they would be able to remember the sounds of letters and how to read words. Trying hard will not help a child with dyslexia. Trouble remembering sounds of letters and combinations of letters are symptoms of dyslexia; more effort is not the solution.

The problems that became obvious in kindergarten became worse in grade 1. When Darryl entered grade 1, he was "a slow starter" in reading and had difficulty with "the ability to distinguish between consonants and detecting rhyming words." His teacher noted, "He is, however, a willing student and should soon overcome this deficiency." Here again the assumption is that if Darryl only tried harder, he would overcome problems stemming from dyslexia. His mother reported reading to him at home and that he enjoyed this reading very much.

From December to April in grade 1, Darryl's report cards noted a "decline in work habits and social skills." His teacher did not seem to realize that because Darryl experienced constant frustration in reading, despite trying hard, he developed difficulty with "self-control" and in accepting responsibility. By April of grade 1, his teacher reported that Darryl did not find "enjoyment in reading," was having reading difficulties, and needed "extra practice." He still had "difficulty with phonics," but he knew most of the consonants.

Interestingly, the picture was not completely bleak. His teacher noted, "Darryl's artwork is above average, and he shows imagination and originality. His printing is very good." As well, his progress in arithmetic was satisfactory. But language difficulties were noted, particularly in the "oral expression of ideas." At the end of grade 1, the teacher reported an improvement in Darryl's reading, but there was still no recognition that Darryl had significant problems that needed special assistance.

Grade 2, Twice Over

Darryl moved on to grade 2 as a "cheerful and eager student." However, he experienced difficulty with reading and with co-operating with other children. Here the difficulties stemming from his dyslexia begin to appear in the form of behavioural problems. Darryl was "not progressing very well, he did not remember from one day to the next and he seems to be unable to settle down and really think about what he is doing." Typical of people with learning disabilities, Darryl would remember the spelling of a word one day and forget it the next. The teacher noted his memory problems, but the school still did not recognize the basis of his reading problem.

At the end of grade 2, Darryl had not progressed significantly, and the school asked him to repeat the grade. Repeating a grade is never the solution, and it can have a very negative effect on a child's self-esteem. Darryl's report card said that he was having difficulty with "word attack" (sounding-out) skills, but he had shown some improvement with initial and final consonants. Vowels were still a big problem. His mathematics was "improving" and his artwork was quite good, but no one recognized his special talent. Today he is an accomplished artist. His errors were interpreted as "careless errors." How cruel! Darryl was not careless; he was trying very hard, in spite of his dyslexia. His teacher noticed that Darryl had "difficulty expressing his thoughts orally" and he did "not speak in sentences." Lack of fluency and incomplete sentences are characteristic of some people with dyslexia.

Darryl's phonics skills were weak, and he was "not yet able to apply these skills to his written work." He had difficulty concentrating and completing his work. He enjoyed discussions in social studies and science, but according to his teacher, "His level of language arts skills hinders his performance in this area." Repeating grade 2 did not help Darryl learn more effectively, and it hurt his self-esteem.

Grades 3 and 4

In grade 3, Darryl's word-attack skills were still "quite weak," although he was beginning to recognize more words. His work in mathematics was acceptable, and he was "an active participant in group discussions and especially likes illustrating in small group enterprises." His "work habits are generally good." The teacher noticed his talent in art and that he was good in music and physical education. Darryl was interested and trying hard, but even these attitudes did not make it possible for him to learn to read. He worked "to the best of his ability this term." His conduct was good. Here we have a picture of a child who is working hard but just cannot read very well—a typical dyslexic.

In grade 4, reading and spelling were still difficult for Darryl. He hated reading out loud. His teacher wrote, "Many of Darryl's errors in spelling are due to his own carelessness." He was not careless; these mistakes indicate a lack of skill that is typical of people with dyslexia.

Darryl had good work habits, but he had some difficulty completing assignments. He was having difficulty in settling down to work, probably because of the terrible frustration that his dyslexia caused.

Grades 5 and 6

In grade 5, Darryl's word-attack skills "improved" but were still well below expectations for his grade, and writing and spelling remained difficult. His work in art was outstanding, and his writing showed creativity and originality, although he still had difficulty with reading and forming letters. Learning to use a computer for word processing is one option that could help a child such as Darryl. Alternatively, if Darryl had been allowed to tell his stories and recite his projects into an audio recorder, then his teachers could have heard the quality of his ideas. He was beginning to have some problems with his social studies projects because of the written work involved, but the teacher noted his "keen interest." His "work habits were generally good" and he was "trying really hard."

When Darryl was in grade 6, the long-term effects of his learning disability became more noticeable. Spelling and reading difficulties continued to plague him. Understandably, he became more and more frustrated, and his attention, concentration, and study habits began to deteriorate. However, his art was still outstanding, he was still "making a good contribution to the discussions," and he was "courteous" and showed "respect." Darryl continued to have difficulty in social studies because of the writing involved, but he seemed to be doing very well in French classes, where the emphasis was on conversation.

Grade 7 and Beyond

In grade 7, Darryl's reading, writing, and spelling difficulties interfered with completing his assignments in French and English, as well as in science and social studies. He received good grades in physical education and in art. A similar pattern continued in grade 8; when he took industrial art in grade 8, he received an A. Throughout this time, he had not received any help for his reading difficulties. In grade 9, Darryl's grades showed a similar pattern.

Throughout secondary school he had difficulty with reading, literature, grammar, and writing. His report card said that "lack of motivation" and "missing classes" were the "cause" of his problems. His dyslexia was not recognized by any of his teachers. Darryl dropped out of school at the end of grade 11. Many years later he completed high school by correspondence.

Recognizing Special Talents

Darryl had some special talents that he was not encouraged to pursue while in school. He could draw very well and had excellent visual-spatial abilities. For example, he could find his way around a new place without getting lost. He could visualize what things looked like from different angles. Studying mechanics at community college, Darryl received a score of 95 per cent and completed a course in heavy-duty mechanics with high grades. He is currently employed as a computer technician.

Darryl's story illustrates very well what happens when reading problems are ignored. He received no diagnosis and no help for his learning disability. He tried hard and was co-operative, but his struggle with reading was a burden that affected his self-esteem. Over time, his frustration led to behavioural problems at school.

Darryl hopes that by sharing his story, the symptoms of learning disabilities will become better known and, as a result, children with the kinds of reading problems he experienced will receive the help they need during their early school years.

There is another side to Darryl's story. Darryl came from a blue-collar family; his father worked in construction and his mother worked as a cleaning woman. Neither completed high school. They did not have the knowledge or confidence to go to the school to demand help for Darryl. Of course, they should not have had to demand help; the teachers and the school should have done much more about his reading difficulties, but they did not. How sad to leave a young child floundering, not giving him the help that he needed. Darryl is not an isolated case. There are thousands of children like Darryl in our school system.

PART III

Coping with a Learning Disability

16

Reading Is a Goose Flying
Learning Disabilities through the Eyes of Children

"Reading is a goose flying. A goose usually doesn't fly but when other birds fly the goose has to follow. The birds go to a higher level then the goose must try to follow but it will be slower."[1] An eleven-year-old boy used this metaphor to write about his dyslexia. He recognized that he would be slower and would have to work harder to catch up to his peers.

In a research project undertaken by Lixian Jin, forty-six children ages eight to fourteen who attended remediation classes at the Dyslexia Association of Singapore were taught about metaphors and asked to write about their dyslexia or other learning problems using metaphors. Through metaphors, these children provide us with special insights about their own perceptions of their learning problems.

Metaphors for Dyslexia

One child wrote, "Dyslexia is a crawling snail because you need time to get used to it and you need time to get to the place you want and you have to sit there and study more time than others. You need to work harder and faster." For another child, dyslexia is "a face that is stress and scared." For another, it is "a broken toilet bowl, everything leaks out . . . If someone comes into your house and sees a broken toilet bowl, what would they think of you. This guy got no money! So stinking and disgusting. . . . People won't like you. . . . I can give them a headache, like fixing a broken toilet is not easy." Some children expressed their anger at their dyslexia: "I want to burn down dyslexia." Dyslexia is "grass that everybody steps on you."

Children with dyslexia often feel different from others, but they long to be the same. One boy poignantly expressed this feeling when he drew two leopards, one with black spots on white background, the other with black spots on black background (a panther). He wrote, "Dyslexia people are the same as other people, but they are like a panther, it is rare, different, but they are the same in the leopard's family."

In the struggle to maintain their self-esteem, the children talked about being good at some subjects in school, even though they could not master reading and mathematics. One boy wrote, "Learning science is a giraffe bending down to eat brown grass, normally a giraffe would eat green grass, but he has to survive by eating brown grass." He felt that he had to be good at something (science) because English and mathematics were not his best subjects.

Metaphors for Reading and Writing

Being slow because of a learning disability and having to work harder than others to get to the same place was a recurring theme with the children in this study. This was especially true for reading. One child wrote that reading makes his head spin.

Some children described reading as a "roller coaster." One of the most frustrating aspects of learning disabilities for parents and teachers, and even for the children themselves, is the variability. On good days, everything seems to go well, but on other days, nothing does. In chapter 22, Susan Hampshire writes about these "ups and downs," a metaphor used by some of the children.

One child wrote that reading is a "book with words that are curly and round like spaghetti, like spaghetti words, curl and round. Non-dyslexic is like so neat while dyslexic is like so untidy." Another child wrote, "Boy doing work with a lot of questions mark on his head. That is a lot of work to do in school and I don't understand what I need to do. Don't understand what my teachers says."

Reading and writing is a "hard rock, because it's very hard to read and very hard to spell," wrote one child. Another child wrote that reading is like "solving a difficult puzzle, because it's hard to get a word when you don't know how to read it." They used striking images about their disability. One child wrote, "Bully— hate bullies makes my face red and makes me burn inside." Another child saw his problem as a "toilet roll—toilet roll can just go roll and roll and roll and roll. You can refill the toilet roll and it will go on and on and on and on."

Some children, despite being dyslexic, find reading rewarding, exciting, engaging, and fun. Their metaphors can help us understand what they enjoy about reading. Some children see pictures in their head when they read. Reading is like "watching a movie, because I think the movie in my head." "When I read, it's like a photo, everything got a picture." Reading can be exciting: like "sailing—fun to play"; like a "roller coaster—it is fast and fun"; like an "action packed movie"; and like "going through an adventure, because reading has an end has a beginning and a story.

And adventure is like reading is because at the end then you know what has happened. It's like a story, at the end you will know what will happen. In the middle is like, what's it called?, suspense? Both reading and adventure have suspense." One child wrote that reading is like a "hot air balloon, I'm raising."

Children used the following metaphors about writing: writing is "walking on a mountain, going up one step at a time"; "climbing Mt Everest, it is hard"; and "egg plant, it is so heavy that I will drop it. It is just like me dropping the pencil because I am so tired." Some children expressed how vulnerable and fragile writing made them feel: "It's like building a card tower, because the sentence structure is hard to master, sometimes and while one mistake, just like a card tower it has this domino effect, you whole sentence is wrong. And people don't like it sometimes. But at the same time it is also fun just like building a card tower you need to have perseverance to build all the way to the top. And your effort maybe all destroyed if you write out of point also. It's like a card tower, everything will fall down if your base, if your foundation is not good everything would come crashing together with it." For another child, writing is like a "volcano—all my writing explodes and come out everywhere. Teacher always say my handwriting is very bad."

Some of the children appeared to have no problem with writing. They described writing as "singing ABC, it is easy"; "a light bulb, it shines imagination"; "jogging in the park, I enjoy it"; and like "wind, it's cool." Students who have handwriting problems are sometimes encouraged to type. One child wrote: "Typing is like a cherry. Easy to eat. . . . Typing is easier than writing because I've learnt how to type and use Microsoft Word brilliantly." For another child, it is "taking a bomb into a battle field: if you know how to utilise writing, you can score a lot of marks. But if you don't know how to use it, it's like a bomb exploding right in your face."

Metaphors for Mathematics, Science, and Computers

For one student, mathematics is a "grape, it has a hard outer layer—which is hard work, something like that. And commitment. Boredom." For others, mathematics is "a storm, it sucks"; like "making a fire, it's hard trying not to get burned"; or like "reading a newspaper, it's boring." One child wrote that math is like "climbing a mountain, because when the teacher just started teaching Maths, you have to sit there and pay attention. So if you don't like it totally, . . . at the end you will lose out, you just fall down from a hill." Like mathematics, science can also be difficult. For one child, learning science is like being "electrocuted, it is hot, uncomfortable." Some students wrote about experiencing joy when they used computers to compensate for their learning problems. One boy wrote that on the computer he felt like a "sports car, I can go very fast."

Lessons from the Children

The children in this study show remarkable insights into their problems and what works for them. They recognize that they are slower and have to work harder than other children, but they can have some satisfying experiences. They long to be like everyone else, but they know that they are different in some ways. We cannot hide or minimize their difficulties or pretend that they are the same as others. I tell them that their brain learns differently, and I always stress their talents. We must allow them to feel valued and to express their frustrations.

17

The Albatross, or Living with a Learning Disability

It has been an albatross around my neck.

—A university student when I asked her what
it was like to have a learning disability

People with learning problems experience terror when asked to read out loud, fill in a form, read a menu, or calculate the tip in a restaurant.[1] It is difficult to imagine what it is like to have a learning disability unless one actually has one. I have had an experience that made me feel the terror. I cannot carry a tune or sing even the simplest song. Once, when I was with a small group of people from all over the world at a professional meeting, each person was asked to sing a song from his or her country. I was petrified and prayed that the earth would open up and swallow me. I broke out in a sweat and turned red in the face. I searched for a way out, finally pleading a non-existent sore throat. For people who can sing, it must be difficult to understand my fear. Fortunately for me, success in school in our society does not depend on the ability to sing. Unfortunately for the people with learning disabilities (many of whom can sing very well), reading, writing, spelling, and mathematics are necessary for success in school and in almost every aspect of their lives.

Reading is critical in our everyday life. People without reading problems take reading for granted; we are not aware of how difficult even the simplest tasks are for those who do not read well. Arithmetic calculations are also part of everyday life: counting change, calculating the tip in a restaurant, figuring out if two cans of tomato sauce at $3.69 are cheaper than buying two cans at $1.89 each. (They are.)

The World of People with Learning Disabilities

"Lazy work. Do it again." "This work is not good enough. Try harder."

Imagine that you are a child in school and you hear these words over and over again. Your teacher or parent who says them scowls and sounds angry. You know that you are trying hard but you cannot seem to understand the mathematics problems or spell the words on the test. You may get angry at the teacher and feel that he or she is picking on you.

Imagine that you are an adult and you have to fill out a form for a credit card application or a mortgage and you cannot understand the instructions or remember your zip or postal code or telephone number. Or you have to write a cheque and cannot remember if the correct spelling is *fourty* or *forty*. How would you feel? Probably stupid and angry with yourself.

Many people experience these situations every day. Writing cheques, filling out forms, remembering telephone numbers, knowing right from left, reading signs while driving, and trying to interpret train timetables can be a nightmare if you have a learning disability.

If you are dyslexic, you have to ask others to read forms and legal papers and ask them to summarize and/or interpret written information. Going to the bank is a stressful experience, particularly if you have long forms or legal documents to read. You face the persistent dilemma of whether to disclose your inability to read the material or just "fake it." A restaurant menu inspires fear not because of the food but because you have to read the menu. People with dyslexia develop coping skills for such situations. They learn to ask the server what the "specials" are, or ask what the ingredients are in some of the more exotic menu items. Or the dyslexic person will wait until everyone else has ordered and then select the item that sounds most appealing.

Even doors can be a problem for people with learning disabilities. One boy reported that as a child he could not distinguish between the words *push* and *pull* on doors. Another person could not read the signs in the subway train stations, especially when there were many people around and it had to be done quickly. A dyslexic can get on the wrong bus by mistaking the sign "Victoria" for the intended destination "Vancouver," or mistaking "New York" for "New Jersey." People with dyslexia often end up in the wrong line or the wrong place because they cannot read the instructions or notices.

Difficulties with finding the correct word can cause problems. One young woman related a story about being in a restaurant and ordering the "long and orange and grows-in-the-ground soup" (carrot soup). Everyone occasionally has this type of word-finding difficulty, but most people with dyslexia experience this quite often.

Some individuals with learning disabilities have problems with finding their way around, often getting lost, and consequently being late for appointments. Some have such severe directional and spatial problems that they can't use public transportation or drive a car.

Other people with a learning disability feel highly anxious whenever they have to go somewhere new. They fear getting lost, being late for an appointment because of it, being embarrassed, and having to apologize or make excuses for their tardiness. Some people learn the adaptive strategy of allowing themselves extra travelling time to compensate for the possibility of getting lost. At the clinic where I work, we are used to people arriving late because they get lost, which disrupts our schedule. We have tried everything—maps, verbal directions, landmarks, and signs—but still people come late. We become as frustrated as the people who are trying hard to find us.

Emotional Pain

Psychologists and educators such as Barbara Riddick, Isabel Shessel, Janice Edwards, Marion Farmer, Christopher Sterling, and Barbara Guyer have interviewed people with learning disabilities and have provided us with a picture of their experiences and feelings. This chapter draws on their work as well as my interviews with children with learning disabilities, their parents, and adults with learning disabilities.

A dark picture emerges. The lives of individuals with learning disabilities are filled with emotional pain, suffering, and feelings of worthlessness and stupidity. They see their experiences in the real world through lenses coloured by their disability. Their daily experiences at school, at home, and at work create an environment that develops and reinforces these feelings. People with learning disabilities have a rough road to travel. Their self-esteem is often low and they experience anger (at themselves as well as others), frustration, depression, and ridicule. The cycle starts with their school experiences and their teachers and extends to their families, peers, and employers, and all the other people they meet in situations where their learning disability becomes obvious.

School Was a Prison

"School was a prison" is how one sixteen-year-old described his school experience. Some people with learning disabilities report having felt lonely and terrified in school. Even when teachers are sympathetic and well meaning, it is sometimes difficult for them to understand how anyone cannot spell simple words or why a student has illegible handwriting. They think that the student is just not trying or is purposefully being difficult.

Many students with learning disabilities have reported that they were terrified when teachers asked them to read out loud or write on the board. They also reported experiencing physical punishment and emotional punishment—shaming, criticism, and anger—when they made mistakes or did not grasp something.

Children with learning disabilities often experience physical abuse as part of their everyday experiences. The physical violence may come from their parents, their teachers, or other children. Students have been punished with canes and rulers and walking sticks. One young man reported that the ruler broke on his hand after the teacher hit him. Others reported being pushed against the classroom wall.

Another child was hit in the face hard during his piano lesson because he could not learn to read the musical notes. It is quite common for individuals with dyslexia to have trouble learning to read musical notes. Musical notes are a symbol system, and people with dyslexia have trouble with any symbol system. However, many people with dyslexia can and do learn to play musical instruments by ear or have good singing voices. Some can eventually learn to read music.

Humiliation

People with dyslexia and other learning disabilities often view school as a place of daily humiliation. Teachers sometimes tell students that they will never be successful at anything. One teacher told a student that he would be lucky to be a garbage collector.

Steve, a high school student with dyslexia, related the following story to me. One day the teacher asked him to hold up a piece of work that he had written. The whole class laughed at the red ink all over the page. One classmate said, "It looks like a rat bled to death all over that paper." Steve learned to hate the sight of red ink and wished that his teachers would use another colour to correct his papers. Another student said that often she wanted to hide in the back of the class or run out of the classroom crying because being humiliated was just too painful.

Students with learning disabilities do not want to be treated differently from the rest of the class. They often feel that they are treated as different, inferior, stupid, and less valuable. Sometimes the rest of the class will pick up cues from the teacher and tease and bully children with learning disabilities and treat them as outcasts. One person stated emphatically that the worst thing a teacher can do to a dyslexic is to embarrass him or her in front of other students.

Sometimes students with learning disabilities are sent to a special room for remedial instruction or are sent to what are called "withdrawal" or "pullout" programs. This, too, can cause embarrassment, as we saw with Johnny in chapter 13. However, some students felt that the special education classes helped them; they felt comfortable there and thought that was where they belonged.

One young woman reported that when she told her teacher that she was dyslexic, her teacher denied that dyslexia exists. This belief is not unusual; even today in our "enlightened" and "sophisticated" age, I have encountered this reaction from some (by no means all) teachers, school principals, and administrators in the school system.

Many people with learning disabilities feel that school let them down. Schools sometimes blamed their problem on bad behaviour or attributed it to an "attitude problem." The school system sometimes ignored their difficulties in the early grades. Some parents recognized the problem, but when they approached the school with their concerns, they were told that they were over-anxious or overprotective or worrying too much. Many children with learning disabilities received no help for their reading, writing, or mathematics disabilities, or, if they did receive help, it was minimal. One man reported that he was given five minutes extra reading time in the corridor twice a week in school. School personnel claimed that he had remedial help every day.

The Class Clown

Having a learning disability can lead to behavioural problems. Students with learning disabilities will often do anything for attention. One man confessed that he was the class leader and troublemaker, causing fights and playing tricks on other students. Other students with learning disabilities became the class clown, making rude gestures when the teacher's back was turned. One student found geography exceptionally difficult. He described how he rigged the map used for geography with fishing lines that could not be seen; in the middle of the lesson, he would pull on the fishing lines and the map would come down on the teacher's head.

Social Pressure

Classmates often manipulate children with learning disabilities; in some cases these children let themselves be manipulated in order to gain approval. To achieve recognition and status from their peers, children with learning disabilities will misbehave and sometimes take the blame for the mischief created by other classmates. One boy took the blame when one of his friends fired an air rifle and shot a hole through a window.

Bullies

Teasing is quite common on the streets and playgrounds where children gather, and sometimes it gets vicious. Children with learning disabilities are often victims of bullies. Bullies tease them, call them "dummy" or "retard" or "slow" or "dumb" or "thick." Sometimes bullies physically attack children with learning disabilities. One man reported being ridiculed for his dyslexia and being asked, "Are you blind?" His classmates teased another boy mercilessly, and when he could not bear to see this happen, he got into a serious fight with thirteen boys against him. He lost.

Problems within Families

School is not the only place where people with learning disabilities encounter problems. Families are not always supportive. Some people reported that their parents were sympathetic but did not really understand the problem. Some felt that their parents were very negative and did not understand the difficulties they experienced. Others reported that their parents tried to help as much as they could. One twenty-year-old woman described very painful early experiences, resulting in a distant relationship with her father. Almost all felt that they were not good enough and had disappointed their parents.

Learning disabilities run in families. A father or mother may have dyslexia or another learning disability that has never been identified. But even that does not always make them sympathetic to the difficulties of their children. Sometimes the parent who has an unidentified learning disability has a great deal of suppressed anger that expresses itself in physical and/or emotional abuse of the child with learning disabilities.

Sometimes brothers and sisters are jealous of the attention that the learning-disabled child receives. Siblings often tease and belittle the child with learning disabilities. One woman remembered her sister telling her that she was "thick and stupid." She hated her sister because she felt that her sister was much cleverer than she was.

Stupid?

"Stupid" is the most frequent word that people with learning disabilities use to describe themselves. As one thirteen-year-old dyslexic girl said, "People just think you are stupid and it makes you feel stupid."

Often people with learning disabilities have very little confidence in themselves. They may try to become invisible by wearing beige clothing and fading into the background. Sometimes they withdraw from contact with other people and feel sad or angry or anxious or depressed—or all of these. They become understandably frustrated when they fail to understand reading or mathematics assignments. Sometimes tears flow. Not everyone with learning disabilities experiences these feelings, but many people do.

One man did not know what his problem was until he was diagnosed with dyslexia at age twenty-three. As a child, he had experienced terrible problems in school and felt that God was punishing him for being bad when he was unable to do the reading, spelling, or mathematics.

When we hear about such feelings, it may be tempting to say, "Stop feeling sorry for yourself" or "It's really not that bad" or "Everyone has problems." But if you do not have a learning disability, it is difficult to understand the daily frustrations, failures, and fears that people with learning disabilities experience.

Self-Doubt and Low Self-Esteem

Lack of confidence is one of the most severe problems for many individuals with a learning disability. Often they blame themselves for their failure, labelling themselves "lazy," "stupid," "dumb," "thick," or "below the other students." One girl saw herself as a "terrible person" whom no one would want as a friend. Another spoke of feeling "devalued as a human being" by her parents' constant negativity.

Some of the people interviewed had such serious emotional problems that they were hospitalized at some point in their lives for emotional breakdowns. Many others received some form of counselling and/or therapy during their lives. Sometimes this was successful, sometimes not.

Anger

People with learning disabilities can become bitter and angry, and their anger can take many forms. We see anger at parents for not being supportive, anger that is sometimes mingled with pain and regret. One woman blamed her parents and professionals for never consulting her in making decisions regarding her life or how she was feeling.

Anger at professionals is rampant, especially anger directed at medical and mental health professionals who misunderstood or misdiagnosed learning problems or failed to provide assistance. Many people expressed anger at educators for embarrassing them in front of other students, not discovering the problem, not recognizing their talents, and not providing the appropriate kind of help—remediation, life skills, accommodations. Their unpleasant experiences at school have filled many people with learning disabilities with anger at parents and professionals and most of all, themselves. Some expressed anger and frustration with having to fight for everything they have achieved.

One woman reported that she left school before completing her education, and she blamed the teachers for not understanding the nature of her learning disability or knowing how to help her. She expressed anger at their "ignorance." Only very recently has she begun to realize that it is also her responsibility to enlighten them.

As mentioned previously, many experienced teachers think that children with learning disabilities are lazy and that their handwriting and spelling are "careless." School, college, and university personnel often put up barriers and roadblocks when people with learning disabilities request accommodations. As an educational psychologist, I have experienced barriers at some universities when I have tried to advocate and get help for students with learning disabilities. Sometimes students are required to get expensive and unnecessarily lengthy psychoeducational assessments. Often professors scoff in disbelief at the idea of a learning disability and do not want to make accommodations in their classes.

For much of their lives, some people with learning disabilities feel that other people do not understand their circumstances.

The Imposter Phenomenon

People with learning disabilities sometimes feel like imposters; if they are successful, they may feel that they are a "phony." They fear that people will find out that they are incompetent and a fraud. They believe that their success is due more to luck and social skills rather than their ability or intellect. The fear of being exposed is overwhelming, and rage and frustration may consume their thoughts.

Stress and Anxiety

Stress and anxiety play a role in every aspect of the lives of almost all people with learning disabilities. Clearly, poor school performance and fear of "looking stupid" are common during school years, and students often pay a price in terms of their health. Some suffer from severe headaches or migraines and neck and back problems from the tension in class.

For most of the participants, the anxiety and stress centre around hiding their learning disability, a fear of exposure, and/or always having to explain their problem to others.

Social Isolation

For several of the participants, social isolation was an unpleasant side effect of "being different." For most, isolation began in childhood; for some, it continued into adulthood. People related painful stories of isolation from parents, siblings, and peers.

One young woman recalled being placed in the "dumb" group in school, which meant that she was separated from the group of kids she socialized with outside school. She and her older sister received tutoring after school for many years, and this kept them from participating in after-school programs. Another woman summarized her feelings of being isolated by saying, "It's almost like, like there's two planets. I'm on this planet and everyone else is on this other planet."

Other participants spoke of being "loners" most of their lives, even if they were married. They preferred to do things alone, or one on one, rather than in groups. Some spoke of their lack of friends during their university years. They all indicated that it was necessary to focus much of their attention and concentration on their studies. There was little time for socializing, and it was not something with which they were particularly comfortable. One student expressed her feelings of isolation when she said, "What's going to happen, who is going to laugh at me today?" Some students felt that life was much better at a special school where everyone had the same problems. There was lighthearted teasing among the students, and since they all shared a problem, there was a sense of camaraderie.

A number of the people interviewed talked about feeling isolated by their learning disability. It either directly interfered in their social lives (as is the case for those with social perception difficulties), or they felt so "different" that they were reluctant to expose themselves to non-learning-disabled people. Some participants specifically stated that they preferred to have other learning-disabled people as friends rather than "normies" because the learning disabled could relate to their life experiences.

One twenty-five-year-old related her experiences of peer rejection at school, including being a target of physical abuse. Another woman reported always feeling out of step with others and unable to relate to her peers. Others reported being unable to participate in many of the games and activities on the school playground.

Hiding behind a Mask

Hiding behind a mask begins early, in first or second grade, when children cannot read what others can. The most common theme is the "mask of invisibility." Individuals who have used this mask said they tried very hard not to be noticed. They would sit at the back of the classroom and try to make themselves small, hoping they could disappear. Several participants recalled that when they were young, they pleaded "with their eyes" for teachers not to pick them to read aloud or answer questions in front of the whole class. One student spoke of the humiliation of spelling tests and his desire to be anonymous. Others hoped and prayed for a fire drill or an earthquake drill so they would not get called on. Some reported that they sometimes saw themselves in the classroom as a cartoon character, shrinking smaller and smaller until they disappeared completely.

Several people spoke of the fear of being "found out"— of other people discovering that they could not write. Some continued to experience that fear of exposure throughout their university years. They never allowed anyone to see the rough drafts of their written work. One woman spoke about hiding her "imperfections." She also noted that from early school to the present she never read out loud. She spoke of not being able to "afford to expose this." Over time her negative self-concept continued to cause her to hide her learning disability. She explained that she spent all her energy hiding her reading problems from others.

Suicide

Depression and suicidal thoughts are often a part of the lives of people with learning disabilities. Most people interviewed admitted to thoughts of suicide and sometimes wanting to die. In a research project in Ontario, Canada, Hazel McBride and I found that all of the adolescent suicides in a three-year period appeared to have had a learning disability that had not been properly identified or treated.[2] We compared the grammar, spelling, and handwriting in adolescent suicide notes with how two groups of students of the same age wrote passages we dictated. One group had a learning disability and the other did not. We found that the grammar, spelling, and handwriting problems the students with a learning disability had were the same as those in the suicide notes. The writing of those students without a learning disability was neat and correctly spelled. Recognizing that the young people who were about to attempt suicide might have been agitated and upset when they wrote their notes, we also examined the notes of a group of older adults who had committed suicide because they were terminally ill and did not want to be a burden to their families. Their suicide notes were neat and often elegant, with carefully chosen language. Based on our research, a learning disability appears to be a significant factor in adolescent suicide, though certainly not the only cause.

The Vicious Cycle

People with learning disabilities often feel embarrassed, hate themselves, feel overwhelmed, and believe that they are failures. They withdraw, become sad and scared, get depressed, and stop trying. This leads to a cycle where everything can get worse. Encouragement, success at something, good remedial help for their disability, and/or sensitive and caring teachers can break this cycle.

Golden Rules for Teachers

Teachers are very important in the lives of children, and even more so in the lives of students with learning disabilities. One student with learning disabilities, Colin Reid, aged seventeen, painted a vivid picture of what it takes to be an awesome teacher.[3]

A good teacher needs passion. "You have to be doing everything as if [it] were a charity. So, you don't hate kids like the people in cartoons that love giving out F's. You need to have a passion, love, dedication to the educational cause, because you are spending your time doing it every day, interacting with hundreds of people. You have to love it."

Very high on his wish list for teachers is the desire and ability to understand each individual student. "Being able to see the situation, being able to see a kid's weaknesses and strengths, their attitude, their personality, their likes and dislikes . . . the best [teachers] should be able to do that."

It is critical for teachers to adapt their teaching to different ways of learning. "If a kid needs a certain way of learning, like touching things and the other kid needs to hear things out loud, the teacher should be able to incorporate everything, every student's personal needs into his class. Even though people often say it is going to be a difficult task to do this, it is often a lot easier than people expect."

Colin had some practical suggestions for teachers. "Shortening your speeches [lectures], writing during your speeches, listing everything that you are talking about, showing movies every now and then. Even those little differences can make a significant difference and have benefits."

Teachers should make sure that each student is learning. "Being able to notice the things going on in the classroom. Some kids may not be doing anything or may be missing things. A teacher should notice it and do something about it."

To teach children with learning disabilities, "You need well educated educators. For example, most teachers I know don't know what a learning disability is. Stuff like this is really important for someone who is going to educate me. They should research more intensely if they [teachers] know that they have students with learning disabilities so they can maximize their ability to learn. Also, you can't send a fresh teacher [beginning teacher] to teach a special needs class. They would not last a minute."

Colin mentioned the importance of patience and persistence. "Being able to do the same thing over and over again . . . and not getting annoyed or ticked off by doing the same thing over and again. A good teacher has to have the quality that allows [him or her] to check the same thing every single time many times a day."

Another important factor is having good student-teacher relationships. "Teachers and kids are more than just an educator and a 'monkey.' It is like a person in your life that you have to deal with for a whole year—a whole year! All those days you are going to see that person. You will either love them or hate them, and the first option is better."

Teachers should be aware of mental health issues. "They should also be able to know and see the signs of depression or anxiety so they [can] intervene before a serious incident happens."

Colin had some advice for teachers. "You are not trying to fail the student. You are trying to get them to succeed. If there is a troublesome student, your purpose is not to ignore them. Your purpose is to help them grow. Even if it feels impossible, it is a challenge that is offered to you. Your challenge as a teacher is to get them to learn. If they pay no attention, then get the kid's attention, if you can."

Colin described some of his favourite teachers. His grade 5/6 teacher "had a no-nonsense attitude. She was persistent in trying to get every person to learn. She was quite honest and thorough. When she made a promise, she kept it. She followed up on her promises, every single one. I learned a lot from her."

He described his grade 10 mathematics teacher as having "amazing teacher-student relationships. He understands how teenagers think. He can almost see through our eyes, in a way. His student-teacher relationships [were] his most prominent feature along with his ability to be interesting."

He really appreciated his grade 11 social studies teacher. "She tries so hard to match your learning needs. She is fairly competent when it comes to learning disabilities and asks questions a lot. She also is willing to adapt to those that don't have special needs. Like if the class hates lectures, then let there be no lectures. Or shorten them out! She is malleable and adaptive."

The Rest of Life

There is more to life than reading, spelling, writing, and mathematics. The challenges of having a learning disability affect all aspects of people's lives, but many have developed some valuable coping strategies. I will describe some of these in the next chapter.

18

Becoming Rhinoceros-Skinned
Learning to Jump the Hurdles

I have painted a negative but realistic picture of the reality of living with a learning disability. However, not all is struggle and sadness. There are some protective factors and coping strategies that help to reduce the powerful effects of constant struggles with academic work.

The work of Isabel Shessel, a learning disabilities specialist, provides valuable insights into coping strategies that people with learning disabilities have developed. For her doctoral thesis, "Adults with Learning Disabilities: Profiles in Survival," she interviewed people with learning disabilities and asked them to reflect on how they learned to live with their learning disability. This chapter highlights some of her research findings.[1]

Advice for Parents

Isabel Shessel found, and my own observations have confirmed, that the strength provided by a loving and supportive family can make the stresses of life far less painful for people with a learning disability. Parents who provide emotional support and encouragement, and who advocate for their children when necessary (until the children are able to do so for themselves), provide an essential resource for children with learning disabilities. At the same time, it is important for parents to encourage children to be independent and self-sufficient. If well-meaning parents are overly protective, children and young adults with learning disabilities may not develop independent living skills because their parents assume they are not capable of doing so.

One young woman Isabel Shessel interviewed said, "I would like to take parents and shake them and say let your child fly as much as he or she is able to, help them, support them, accommodate them if necessary, do battle for them, if you must, with the educational system, but for heaven sakes don't cocoon them, because you end up with a tragic situation."[2]

Another young woman reported that she had "smothering" parents. She had a terrible sense of direction, and her parents were afraid for her and unwilling to teach her how to get around in the city on her own. Another woman referred to her house as a "war zone." Her mother set extremely high standards of behaviour, and the girl learned early in life "not to expose" her weaknesses within her family. She knew that to do so would mean being belittled and berated for "not trying hard enough."

A family that values co-operation with the school and works with the school can be a tremendous help. Parents who recognize a learning disability at a relatively early age and work with (or sometimes even fight) the school system can make a big difference. Intensive intervention in the elementary school years is essential for children with learning disabilities to develop self-esteem.

Prescription for Professionals

Assisting people with learning disabilities involves understanding that a learning disability is not just an educational issue. Helping them to understand their personal strengths and weaknesses is critical, both in developing self-esteem and in making career choices. Discovering areas of strength and focusing on strengths rather than weaknesses are particularly important in making good career choices. Isabel Shessel's research participants identified a need for more career counselling for people with a learning disability while they are in school. Networks where parents and professionals can communicate with each other are also valuable. Two such networks are LDonline (www.ldonline.org) and LDExperience (www.ldexperience.ca).

One student in Shessel's study suggested that it would be valuable to offer in-service training on various types of disabilities and disability issues for medical and mental health professionals, social workers, and educators. Such courses should also be incorporated into the accreditation process for such professionals.

Homework for Educators

Educators have a responsibility to create safe classroom environments for all students, including those with a learning disability. All students should be encouraged to ask questions when they do not understand something. I have a rule in my classes: there are no stupid questions. I let my students decide if my answers are stupid. If they answer questions incorrectly, they should never be humiliated. Fear of humiliation makes being creative and thoughtful particularly difficult for people with a learning disability.

Many of the participants in Shessel's study were able to trace their negative self-concepts back to their earliest experiences in school when they were humiliated. Educators should be encouraged to make education fun, to be creative, and to use alternative ways of teaching. Universal Design for Learning (UDL) is an educational approach that recognizes that people comprehend information in different ways. For example, some people remember more information when it is presented visually; others prefer to hear it. Think of yourself at a lecture. Would you rather read the information or hear it? UDL encourages educators to use multiple ways of presenting information. UDL also recognizes that there are many ways of representing what you know. Some people would rather write a paper; others would rather draw a diagram or present orally. Training teachers to be aware of these multiple modalities is important.

Life beyond the Classroom

Educators should prepare people for life outside the classroom. Some people with learning disabilities have had remedial assistance and classroom accommodations while they were in school. Although this help is important, it does little to prepare them for the realities of the workplace.

As one law student explained, "If all you've ever done is go to school, you can't know what the rest of the world is like."[3] His education did not prepare him for the practical realities of his chosen profession. He needed an education in managing people, money, and the multiple demands on his time, all of which can be serious problems for people with learning disabilities. Several interviewees noted the need for mentors in the workplace to provide feedback (positive and negative) about how a person is doing, especially when starting a new job.

Reading, writing, mathematics, and spelling are obviously important, but they are not everything. Some students in Isabel Shessel's study indicated that there was such a strong emphasis on dealing with the educational aspects of their learning disability that they were not given the opportunity to develop social skills and coping strategies such as self-advocacy. Learning to "consider all the options," to "brainstorm the possibilities," and to develop alternate plans are important skills that more people with learning disabilities should get experience with during their schooling.

Survival Skills

All is not bleak for those with learning disabilities; many develop creative survival skills. Among the survival skills Shessel identified from her research are the following: persistence, self-advocacy, teamwork, assuming responsibility, learning to ask for help, humour, developing a positive outlook on life, and appreciating different ways of learning.

Persistence: Becoming Rhinoceros-Skinned

Persistence is one of the most striking characteristics of successful adults with learning disabilities. Often they discover that they have to work longer and harder than others simply to keep up, and this determination becomes a way of life. *Cannot* is not in their vocabulary. One man described his recipe for success: "You have to be thick-skinned, rhinoceros-skinned, elephant-skinned. You can't internalize failures; you have got to learn from them." [4]

Self-Advocacy

For many of the participants in Shessel's study, "believing in themselves" and advocating for their rights and needs were crucial components of survival. Learning to tell others that they had a disability and needed accommodation when pursuing higher education and in the workplace was key in some cases. One man said, "If I hadn't been able to stand up for myself, nobody else would have."[5] His survival depended on understanding his own needs and being able to stand up to his superiors when he felt that his needs were not being met or his rights were being denied. Developing effective self-advocacy skills contributed to achieving a sense of control over their lives, which is important for people with a learning disability.

Disclosing that you have a learning disability is part of advocating for yourself, but it is best done in a safe environment where you will not be penalized or denigrated. One of the dilemmas that people with learning disabilities face is whether and/or when to tell people about their problem. Some people are sympathetic when they are told, but one man described "the look of horror on his face" when he told one teacher.

Isabel Shessel found that many of the people she interviewed were reluctant to disclose their learning disabilities. They reported experiences of prejudice and discrimination related to disclosure of their learning disabilities. For most it was in the workplace, but for a few it involved academic institutions, particularly universities.[6] I have met a number of university professors who deny that there are learning disabilities and insist that it is just laziness. When one man told a professor at university that he was learning disabled, the professor, who was outspoken about his belief that learning disabilities do not exist, responded that he was using the label as an excuse to get a computer. When some people hear that a person is dyslexic, they view it as an excuse to get special privileges, like the boy in an earlier chapter who thought that because he had dyslexia he did not have to clean up his room.

Some study participants said they constantly had to explain the nature of their learning disability and their particular needs to every new supervisor at work. Others reported that some people ask, "When will you get better?" Sometimes disclosing dyslexia backfires; people tell jokes that make fun of people with dyslexia or other learning disabilities. These jokes hurt. Other people's views of people with a learning disability can be as big a problem as the disability itself.

One young woman struggled for several years to gain admission to graduate school. When she first applied, she thought that it would be in her best interest to identify herself as a person with a learning disability, so she indicated that she had problems with written expression. When she was not accepted into the program, she questioned the admissions personnel. They responded, unsympathetically, that given the kinds of problems she had, if she were on the admissions committee, would she want a student like herself in their class?

Teamwork

Learning to ask others for help is critical. All of the people interviewed reported that having somebody to talk to or a support group who understands learning disabilities is very helpful. Many students prefer working in a group. As you will read in chapter 23, Greg Louganis reported that at university, he found it much easier to absorb the material when he worked with a group. When he was attending an educational institution that did not encourage group work, his struggles with his studies increased significantly.

Many participants in Isabel Shessel's study indicated that they teamed up with other students who were good readers and had them read the material out loud. One learning-disabled student who was strong in mathematics asked another student to read the math questions so she could solve the problems. Some research participants recounted asking others to do writing for them (both in school and in the workplace) until they felt comfortable to attempt it themselves. Several participants developed reciprocal support networks with friends and co-workers. "So you find if you can't do something, you find someone to do the job for you. And you do the job that you're good at."[7]

Johnny, in chapter 13, helped a student learn to dance in exchange for getting help with chemistry. John Corcoran, in chapter 14, also managed to get people to do things for him. Focusing their attention and energy on what they can do rather than on what they cannot do is a useful survival strategy for people with learning disabilities.

Assuming Responsibility

The participants in Isabel Shessel's study spoke about their frustrations—as children and as adults—with being dependent on others for certain kinds of assistance. Some felt they were not participants in their own life decisions, and they struggled to gain control over their lives. The severity of one student's reading disability made it necessary for him to have others do his reading for him. He spoke about feeling like a "user" because he was always asking someone to do something for him. When describing his experiences as a university student, he said, "There's this blurring of what is yours and what is theirs . . . Is this really my essay or is this their essay with some of my ideas?"[8] He even questioned his friendships, at times asking himself, "Do you really like this person or are you being nice to this person because you need him?"[9] For this man, the fear of depending on other people contributed to his anxiety.

Learning to Ask for Help

Asking for help was one of the most difficult tasks for many people Isabel Shessel interviewed. Asking for help meant exposing their weaknesses; it led to embarrassment and shame. Some study participants attempted to cope by "just trying harder" and not asking for help. The balance between learning to strive for independence and learning to ask for help is precarious. Some study participants had come to terms with their need to ask for assistance. As one person explained, "One of the smartest things I've ever learned is that, I don't have to have all the information. I just have to know where to get the information."[10] Another person expressed the view that it is fine to ask for help "because you will be able to help someone at a later time."[11]

For many people with learning disabilities, the key to success was making conscious decisions to take charge of their lives and making adaptations in order to move ahead. Knowing the rights of people with disabilities also helped some individuals achieve a sense of empowerment. Technological advances—including computers, portable spell-checkers, and audio recorders—have enabled many people with a learning disability to be more independent in their daily living and in the workplace. One man who used a voice-activated computer and word-processing software that assisted with his writing and spelling reported that this technology enabled him to function more independently in his job and to feel more control over his life.

Humour

"I use a lot of humour as a survival strategy, because if you can't laugh at yourself, who can you laugh at?" one young woman told Isabel Shessel. For her, humour is "an important catharsis." A good laugh breaks up the anxiety for her because "you can't be anxious when you're laughing."[12]

Another person said, "You can't take yourself so seriously that every little so-called failure is a big issue."[13] Humour is a stress reducer, and it can also help with remembering information (for example, by creating a funny image that can be remembered more easily). According to one student, "If you cannot laugh at yourself then life can become very frustrating. You have to find a way to diffuse the frustration."[14] For him, humour makes the frustrations livable. If used appropriately, humour can relieve tension and create a good atmosphere. However, there is also a negative side to humour if it involves putting oneself down.

Finding the Positives

Many participants in Isabel Shessel's research expressed a desire to focus on positives rather than negatives in terms of dealing with the ups and downs on life's journey. One woman defined a disability as "anything stopping you from being the best you can," but she expressed the sentiment that you should not let a disability take over your life.[15] One professional woman who developed many positive ways of dealing with setbacks said her approach to life was "If you can't do one thing, another door will open."[16]

One clever young woman became adept at changing people's negative comments about learning disabilities into positives. "If people say 'you're hyperactive,' I say, 'no, I just don't get tired easily.' If people say 'you're disorganized,' I say, 'I view things from many points of view at the same time.'"[17] Some study participants advised others to view negative experiences as learning opportunities: figure out what you did wrong and how you can improve for the next time.

Emotional well-being is a key factor in successful survival. "Learning disabled people really need to be healthy emotionally and nurture themselves," said one study participant.[18] Others emphasized "believing in yourself," "learning to like who and what you are," "not being afraid to ask for help when you need it," and "[never] being ashamed of your learning disability."

The people with learning disabilities who were interviewed identified the following ways in which being learning disabled had a positive impact on their lives: it helped them be a better person through facing the hurdles and frustration of their lives; it allowed them to think creatively; it increased their sensitivity to others and made them more caring and considerate; and it developed in them the desire to help others. One person noted, "My listening skills, my compassion, my ability to think on my feet, to problem solve, to do so many things, I think have been challenged and become much stronger because of my disability than if I didn't have it."[19] One woman used her creativity, love of learning, and negative memories of her own education to become an innovative and widely praised educational consultant.

Speaking about her negative experiences in school, one woman revealed that she wanted to be the type of teacher that she always wished that she could have but never did. Looking back at what she struggled with in school made her determined to help other children to reach their potential. For another woman, the terror that she had felt in school made her want to give all children, especially those with learning problems, the best education that she could.

People with learning disabilities value the ability to problem-solve in creative ways. When asked if she would get rid of her learning disability if she could, one woman emphatically said that she would not. "It has allowed me to grow in ways other people cannot. . . . I'm used to doing things differently cause I always had to find my own strategies," she said.[20] Another woman spoke of learning to see several possible solutions to problems and not seeing things as black or white as her coping strategy.

The participants in the study identified the desire to help others as another positive impact of having a learning disability. Careers that involve helping others, such as health care, mental health, or disability advocacy, appealed to some research participants because they believed that others could benefit from their experiences and advice. "My goal in life is to help people reach their full potential," said one student. Another person noted, "The biggest battle of all with dyslexics is for their self-esteem. They feel stupid. They have been treated as stupid."[21]

Isabel Shessel found that many people with a learning disability "struggled to accept themselves as valuable human beings."[22] Denial of their learning disabilities was a maladaptive strategy that a number of study participants used. For some, denial led to stress, poor health, and even hospitalization. Some study participants tried for years to cover up their learning problems. Others realized that by developing positive self-esteem, they could accept their learning differences and find creative ways to adapt. Encouraging children in the development of their talents is very important. If people with learning disabilities have musical or artistic or athletic talent and these abilities are recognized and fostered, other children (and teachers) will admire them and value their abilities, which will help develop their self-esteem.

The Road to Self-Esteem

Isabel Shessel has made a valuable contribution by helping us understand the coping mechanisms of people with learning disabilities. Written with empathy and understanding, her work emphasizes guarded optimism that people with learning disabilities can cope with their disabilities. But she makes it clear that we cannot minimize or discount the struggles. Most of all, we must recognize that people with learning disabilities are not objects but individuals with hopes and dreams and successes and failures. They are both victims and survivors.

19

"School Sick"
Avoiding Detection

Many children with learning disabilities hate school. Some may go to extraordinary lengths to avoid it, pretending to be ill to escape having to go to school.

Thomas Mann, a celebrated German writer (1875–1955), captures such deceptions in his brilliant novel *Confessions of Felix Krull, Confidence Man*. Filled with humour and irony, this novel provides some revealing insights into the clever (or not-so-clever) techniques frequently used by children with learning problems so that they can avoid school.

The central character in Mann's novel, Felix Krull, is a smug, self-centred, pretentious man who has no feeling for anyone but himself. Felix is not identified as having dyslexia (the terms dyslexia or learning disabilities were not in the popular consciousness at the time that Thomas Mann wrote the book), but there are clues in the novel that he does. For example, Felix is "backward in school" and could not finish it. He has some sort of language deficit and reports that "verbal communication is not my element." Similar to most people with learning disabilities, Felix has some severe memory lapses. However, he has a good visual memory and remembered the details of an operetta years after he saw it.

Felix is filled with hatred of school; he describes it as a "malignant institution." He writes that school was worse than the prison in which he was later incarcerated. School was a place of slavery and fear. He soon looked for ways to escape from school, including feigning illness. His mysterious illnesses never occurred on Sundays and holidays.

Felix decided to forge his father's handwriting, not only for his own amusement but in the interests of his "intellectual freedom." One forged note detailed his severe stomach pains and another explained that he had a gumboil and a sprained right arm. Of course, these imaginary ailments required Felix to stay home from school.

In addition to forging notes, Felix became quite adept at feigning illness. He learned that he could precipitate an attack of chills and chattering teeth by throwing off the bed covers and lying in the cold room for a few minutes. To add to the "illness," he pulled in his cheeks and held them in with his teeth, which made his chin disappear. He would also twitch his eyes and dilate his nostrils, making himself look quite sick.

Huddled in his bed with his blue fingers across his chest and his teeth chattering, he waited patiently for his mother to find him. When she came to look for him, he told her he was sick— he had headaches; he was cold. He was fed a diet of porridge and dry toast, and sometimes even refused food, which helped his mother believe that he really was sick. He pretended to vomit but could not; he claimed that he had thrown up all night. When his mother decided to call the doctor, he secretly rejoiced. Although he was initially afraid that the doctor would see through his ruse, he discovered that doctors were easily fooled. Of course, Felix presented quite a challenge for the doctor, because his "symptoms" did not follow any typical pattern. His "illness" was sometimes diagnosed as a migraine, sometimes as the flu. When Felix asked the doctor what was wrong, the doctor would wink, smile, or pause briefly, trying to encourage Felix to admit that he was playing "school sick." Felix persisted in playing this game. He may not have excelled in school, but he certainly was an expert at avoiding it.

Thomas Mann died before completing *Confessions of Felix Krull, Confidence Man* or writing the sequel he had planned. The novel was nonetheless published, first in German in 1954 and a year later in English. Although Mann depicts Felix as a con artist and mentions several references to Felix being in prison, the novel does not explain why he went to prison. Of course, most people with dyslexia do not become con artists, but Felix's story illustrates how difficulties in school, if not recognized and if the child is not helped, can contribute to the making of a very disturbed individual.

Like the fictional character Felix, students with learning disabilities often pretend to be sick to avoid school. One girl reported trying to break her arm so she would not have to write an examination. Another girl jabbed a pencil through her hand. One twelve-year-old developed a "pain" in his leg so he would not have to go to school. Another child used to fake migraines, stomach aches, and sore arms. He created infected bruises by banging against furniture or getting into fights. He would make himself vomit by sticking his fingers down his throat, and he demanded medication for false headaches and stomach pains. He would even eat cat food to become sick. He especially used these avoidance techniques on days when school tests were scheduled.

Forging notes from parents was a common ruse. Only the cleverer students were capable of this deception; most teachers recognized the signs of an amateur forgery. Getting involved in fights could result in two or three days of suspension from school and, not surprisingly, this strategy was occasionally used. Running away from school was another tactic.

In the classroom, students with learning difficulties use other "clever" techniques to avoid detection. Some try to hide spelling problems by writing so small that no one can see the spelling. To escape reading aloud, students "forget" their books or pretend to lose their place. Teachers can, of course, see right through these deceptions.

Thomas Mann and other writers have given us a picture of the emotional life of people with dyslexia and their difficulties in school and in everyday life. My own observations and those of other psychologists and educators have shown how common being "school sick" is among children with learning disabilities.

Parents need to be aware that stomach aches and vague complaints of not feeling well may be a sign of a learning disability. If parents notice this "school sickness" especially on Mondays or on the days of spelling or mathematics tests, then they should investigate further. Of course, the child could have the flu or a virus, but there is a significant chance that "school sickness" could be a sign of a learning disability.

20

Dyslexia and Murder?

"Eunice Parchman killed the Coverdale family because she could not read or write."[1] This sentence appears at the beginning of *A Judgement in Stone*, a novel by the noted British mystery and crime writer Ruth Rendell. This novel is an intriguing account of the thoughts and actions of a dyslexic character, Eunice Parchman, as she attempts to live in the modern world where reading is essential to everyday life. Rendell leads us on a fascinating journey into the mind of a dyslexic, and with the skill of a specialist in learning disabilities (which Rendell is not), helps us understand dyslexia from the point of view of someone afflicted with this problem.

A word to Ruth Rendell fans and mystery aficionados in general: in this discussion of *A Judgement in Stone* I do not reveal any critical elements of the plot. The reader knows from the beginning of the novel that Eunice Parchman committed the crime. The plot is a gradual and suspenseful crescendo to the inevitable climax of the story.

Dyslexia and Problems in Daily Life

People with dyslexia have problems in everyday life. Eunice was no exception. Rendell skilfully depicts these difficulties. When Eunice wants to take a train to her new job, she cannot read the board with the information about the trains and is forced to ask someone. This person gives her the information but taunts her. "'Which platform for Stantwich?' 'It's up on the board, lady. Thirteen. Can't you read?'"[2]

The challenges of everyday living for dyslexics become really obvious when Eunice goes to work as a servant for a family called the Coverdales. In her job, she encounters notes, shopping lists, and papers, all of which she must pretend to read but cannot. Eunice finds herself working for a very literate family, consisting of George, the husband; Jacqueline, the wife; and the two children, Melinda and Giles. The adolescent son, Giles, reads all the time, even at the dinner table. The family is very well educated, and the lady of the house is horrified at the quality of the handwriting in the letter that Eunice "wrote" in response to the advertisement for household help. Of course, Eunice did not really write the letter; the clever manipulation that she used to get the position is an example of the subterfuge that people with dyslexia may be forced to use.

The family is perplexed because Eunice "rudely" ignores notes that they occasionally leave for her. She is terrified of these notes. Rendell writes: "She was as frightened of those pieces of paper as another woman would have been had Giles kept a snake in his room."[3]

A crisis arises when Eunice receives a telephone call from her employer asking her to find some notes he left on the desk. Because of her illiteracy, she is unable to locate the missing papers. She eventually just hangs up the phone and ignores its insistent ringing because she is unable to explain why she cannot find the papers. This particular incident is a catalyst for her actions that follow: "The incident of the Coverdale History papers had made her retreat totally into her shell, for if she were to speak or allow them to speak to her, that arch enemy of hers, the printed word, would rise up and assail her. Reading in an armchair pulled close to a radiator, reading to please Eunice and keep clear of her, Jacqueline never guessed that she could have done nothing to please Eunice less or arouse her more to hatred."[4]

At one point, a family member tries, in all innocence, to get Eunice to read a quiz in a magazine. Eunice is trapped and lashes out like a wild animal. Rendell writes: "She understood only that she was on the brink of having her disability discovered, and because of the awful crushing domination of that disability, she thought she was nearer to that brink than she actually was."[5]

The daughter, Melinda, discovers that Eunice's glasses are made of plain glass. "Her eyes went to Eunice's flushed face, her blank stare, and pieces of the puzzle, hitherto inexplicable—the way she never read a book, looked at a paper, left a note, got a letter—fell into place. 'Miss Parchman,' she said quietly, 'are you dyslexic?'"[6] Melinda's realization has profound consequences (which I will leave for readers of the novel to discover) because it means that the family now knows Eunice's secret.

Later her employer confronts her and taunts her for not being able to read. This is the kind of teasing that people with dyslexia experience in everyday life. "Her flush and the distortion of her face told him he had gone too far under gross provocation. He had committed that most uncouth of sins, mocked the hunchback's hump."[7]

One can sense Eunice's gradual buildup of resentment against this family. "Lowfield Hall was full of books. It seemed to Eunice that there were as many books here as in Tooting Public Library where once, and only once, she had been to return an overdue novel of Mrs. Samson's. She saw them as small flatfish boxes, packed with mystery and threat. One entire wall of the morning room was filled with bookshelves; in the drawing room great glass-fronted bookcases stood on either side of the fireplace and more shelves filled the twin alcoves. There were books on bedside tables, magazines and newspapers in racks. And they read books all the time. It seemed to her that they must read to provoke her, for no one, not even schoolteachers, could read that much for pleasure."[8]

Over time, a disturbing conflict occurred between Eunice and the family; her resentment of the family boiled up and became a lethal hatred. They were no longer people to Eunice; in her mind they became the printed word. "They were those things in the bookcases, those patchy black blocks on white paper, eternally her enemies, hated and desired."[9]

As Rendell notes, "It was unfortunate for Eunice Parchman, and for them, that the people who employed her and in whose home she lived for nine months were peculiarly literate. Had they been a family of philistines, they might be alive today and Eunice free in her mysterious dark freedom of sensation and instinct and blank absence of the printed word."[10] Having to live with the scorn of others and hiding the fact that she could not read created emotional scars in Eunice that led to tragic consequences.

Emotional Aspects of Dyslexia

The attitudes of society to those who cannot read contribute to the lack of self-esteem and other emotional problems that people with dyslexia often experience. Ruth Rendell uses the character of Eunice to illustrate this. Eunice became indifferent to people as a defence for her reading problem. Rendell writes: "The printed word was horrible to her, a personal threat to her. Keep away from it, avoid it, and from all those who will show it to her. The habit of shunning it was ingrained in her; it was no longer conscious. All the springs of warmth and outgoing affection and human enthusiasm had been dried up long ago by it. Isolating herself was natural now, and she was not aware that it had begun by isolating herself from print and books and handwriting."[11] When Eunice is left alone after her parents have died, she lives by herself, without contact with people. She develops a cold, insensitive personality.

Eunice does not make friends easily because of her emotional problems and her fear of her illiteracy being discovered. "Illiteracy had dried up her sympathy and atrophied her imagination. That, along with what psychologists call *affect*, the ability to care about the feelings of others, had no place in her make-up."[12] As a result, a "friend" can easily dominate Eunice and lead her astray. This so-called friend helps Eunice decode the notes that the family leaves for her and carefully leads the unsuspecting servant into a terrible crime.

The Hidden Disability

People who have dyslexia or any kind of learning disability often experience feelings of shame. This was certainly true for Eunice. Learning disabilities are not obvious, such as blindness or deafness or the inability to walk. This lack of visibility is problematic because other people often view people with learning disabilities as stupid or lazy. Even today, society does not really understand people with dyslexia.

Eunice Parchman's greatest fear was that her reading problem would be discovered and, thus, she went to great lengths to hide her dyslexia. In the end, however, she experiences the ultimate humiliation—the judge at her trial exposes her problem to the world. The secret that she kept from the world and that she would kill for to preserve was revealed.

It is reasonable to ask why Eunice's dyslexia was not diagnosed and why she did not receive help when she was in school. Eunice would have been in elementary school in the 1940s, when the word *dyslexic* was not widely used or in the public consciousness. She had difficulty learning to read as a child, but she was from a blue-collar family that lacked money for private diagnosis or tutoring. In that era, wealthier families might have used private means to help their "problem" children who did poorly in school, and their children might also have received special attention in school, but such help was not given to children from lower-class families such Eunice's.

Media reports of statements by an occasional psychologist have sometimes led to the public misperception that dyslexics are all quite intelligent and have special talents. Rendell did not fall into the trap of accepting this stereotype; clearly, Eunice does not fit this image. She was poor, and not particularly bright, and had no special talents to help her compensate for her severe problems with reading. When Ruth Rendell wrote this book, the prevailing idea about dyslexics among professionals and the public was that it was a problem of visual perception (for example, seeing and writing letters backwards). Her analysis was much deeper and closer to the truth, indicating that she was years ahead of her time. We now know that dyslexia is a language problem.

Coping with Dyslexia

Throughout the novel, Eunice uses various techniques to cope with her dyslexia. For example, she pretends to be unable to read something because she does not have her glasses with her. Subsequently, the Coverdale family arranges for her to get a pair of glasses, so this strategy fails miserably. When Eunice gets the glasses, Rendell writes: "In them she felt a fool. Must she wear them all the time now, she who could see the feathers on a sparrow's wing in the orchard a hundred feet away? And would they expect her to *read*?" Of course, the glasses do not help her read. "But now, with the glasses in her possession, occasionally even on her nose, she became very aware of the printed word which surrounded her and to which, at some future time, she might be expected to react."[13]

When this book was written, there was nothing in the scientific literature about the compensatory mechanisms that are accessible to people with dyslexia, yet Rendell appears to have been aware of them. She describes Eunice's excellent visual memory. Because of her memory, Eunice is able to recognize an illegal act and uses this knowledge to blackmail a neighbour to obtain money. When Eunice is given a list of groceries, which of course she cannot read, she uses the ingenious technique of asking her friend to read her the list (because she "forgot" her glasses). Eunice's memory allows her to remember the information after hearing the items only once. When she is in church, Eunice cannot read the hymn sheets, but if she hears a hymn once she remembers it and can sing with a lovely voice. Although she cannot read a knitting pattern, Eunice is also able to knit lovely sweaters. How does she do it? She has excellent artistic skills and learns to use her visual memory because she cannot rely on print.

Literacy and Society

The central thesis of this novel is that the ability to read helps control our baser instincts. The printed word acts as a device to tame humanity. "Literacy is one of the cornerstones of civilization. To be illiterate is to be deformed. And the derision that was once directed at the physical freak may, perhaps more justly, descend upon the illiterate." Rendell echoes what she considered to be societal beliefs in the 1970s: people with dyslexia are somehow not normal, and individuals who cannot, or do not, read are not quite human. She writes, "And yet, although her companion and partner was mad, Eunice was not. She had the awful practical sanity of the atavistic ape disguised as twentieth-century woman."[14]

Print materials give us abstractions and allow us to use our imaginations and enter into the past or the future. Eunice, deprived of print, lived only in the present, never thinking about the past or the future.

Rendell speculates whether watching violent television programs was a factor in Eunice's crime. "Thus it happened that the first programme Eunice ever saw on her own television dealt with violence and with firearms. Did it and its many successors stimulate her latent violence and trigger off waves of aggression? Did fictional drama take root in the mind of the illiterate so that it at last bore terrible fruit?"[15]

Research findings support Rendell's hypothesis. There is a relationship between the amount of violence an individual watches on television and aggressive and anti-social behaviour.[16] One of the hypotheses Rendell proposes is that watching television does not allow the use of the imagination in the way that reading print materials does. When you read about a character or a scene in a book, you must imagine what it looks like. When you watch violence on television, it becomes quite vivid and real, whereas reading requires imagination and allows you to develop an understanding of the difference between fantasy and reality. Therefore, there may be a causal connection between television viewing and violent acts. However, Rendell also notes that Eunice committed violent acts before she watched violent programs on television, so television alone cannot be blamed for her criminal act.

A Writer's Insights, and a Warning

Ruth Rendell has written a sensitive and perceptive account of dyslexia. This novel presents one of the clearest arguments for early detection and treatment of learning disabilities, and it promotes greater understanding of individuals who have learning disabilities. With her skills as an observer of human behaviour, Rendell probes and dissects the anguish, hopelessness, terror, loneliness, anger, and self-hatred of individuals who cannot read. She clearly portrays what it feels like to be dyslexic and the difficulties in everyday life that accompany dyslexia.

The question I asked myself was, how did Rendell come to know so much about dyslexics? How did she, who was not an educator or a psychologist, develop such detailed insights into dyslexia? I have not found an answer to this mystery, although I have searched for biographical information about Rendell. I learned that she was a journalist before she became a mystery writer, but she had no special training in the field of education.

Rendell provided one clue in a letter to me. She wrote, "I knew nothing about dyslexia when I wrote *A Judgement in Stone*. The character of Eunice Parchman came entirely out of my imagination. I do not, in fact, think it very difficult for the ordinary person of average sensitivity to imagine what it must be like to be unable to read. I imagined that and I did what I always do when creating a character very unlike myself—get into their skin, take on their background and proceed from there."[17]

I found another clue in a published interview with Rendell: "I give it a lot of thought before I start writing, and when I am writing I think myself into the character, I become that character. So that I think, I am this person, and what would I do next in the circumstances?"[18]

A Judgement in Stone can be seen as a warning. Eunice's self-loathing, anguish, and anger at the world fuelled her passions and blinded her logic. If we do not pay attention to people with dyslexia and other learning disabilities and help them, we may see more individuals such as Eunice Parchman, and we may face more tragedies such as the fictional one in this book.

Dyslexia and Murder: A Causal Connection?

Rendell makes us wonder who or what is responsible for the terrible act of murder described in this novel. Are the education and social systems responsible because they failed to identify Eunice's problem when she was a child and did not try to help her? Are the people who mocked her and destroyed her self-esteem responsible? Are the violent television programs that she watched, which blurred her understanding of the difference between fantasy and real life, responsible? Or are all of these factors implicated? There are no easy answers to these questions.

Does having dyslexia cause people to commit murder? Of course not. Dyslexia does not cause people to become criminals, and it is not an excuse for a criminal act. But having to live with the scorn of others and hiding the fact that they cannot read can create emotional scars that may lead to serious consequences for individuals and for society.

This novel's messages are profound. Society must recognize and treat dyslexia early on, before secondary emotional problems develop. Reading civilizes us. Reading is a path to communication with others, a means to allow us to use our imagination, and a bridge to another world. Reading allows us to leave ourselves and join the world of others.

If we want to prevent terrible acts such as the one Ruth Rendell depicts in *A Judgement in Stone*, we must recognize and address learning disabilities in all children and adults who have them.

21

A Parent's Worst Nightmare

Ellen Edwards screamed when she saw her son Jason on fire.[1] Yellow flames, blue in the centre, were shooting out from his face and body. She ran for a hose, sprayed water on him, hearing his cries of pain echoing in her ears. The smell of burning flesh filled the air.

Minutes earlier, Jason had doused himself with gasoline, lit a match, and set himself on fire. Third-degree burns covered most of his body. Jason lived for ten days in the burn unit of a local hospital before he died.

The seeds of Jason's horrific suicide were sown years earlier when he had trouble learning to read in grade 1. His mother asked the school to give him extra help to improve his reading. The school told her not to worry; children mature at different rates and he would catch up. She was a single parent, and the school implied that she was the cause of the problem: she worried too much, she was overprotective, and she did not read to him enough. What the school told Ms. Edwards is simply nonsense.

We know that simply reading to children will not prevent dyslexia. Living in a single-parent family does not cause dyslexia. There are many two-parent families with dyslexic children.

Jason did not catch up in grade 2 or grade 3. He struggled with reading and spelling, and his handwriting was impossible to read. However, he was energetic, motivated, and popular with his elementary school classmates.

In grade 4, Jason finally received an assessment to see if he had a learning disability. Unfortunately, the assessment was woefully inadequate and did not include the important tests that I describe in chapter 11. Jason's assessment consisted of an IQ test, a test of eye-hand coordination, and a test of his memory for words. He was not given a reading test, a pseudoword reading test, or spelling or mathematics tests. According to the report, Jason showed *no* evidence of a learning disability.

In elementary school, he saw the school counsellor once a week for disruptive behaviour, but he received no help for his reading. Throughout Jason's schooling, his reading difficulties remained unaddressed. Instead, school personnel asserted that his reading and spelling problems were caused by his "bad behaviour," not as a result of a learning disability.

Upon entering high school in grade 9, Jason had major difficulties and did not pass at the end of that school year. The school still did not test him further to determine whether he had a learning disability. By the end of grade 10, he had an emotional breakdown and was hospitalized. When he was in grade 11, I tested Jason and determined that he had dyslexia. His reading and spelling were well below average for his age and grade. His handwriting had poorly formed letters and was nearly impossible to read. However, his scores on mathematics tests were in the average range. On a test measuring visual-spatial skills, he scored in the highest level. He was a genius with computers. In addition, he was a talented artist and musician and a thoughtful and caring person. I recommended to the school authorities that he receive help for his reading, spelling, and writing, and I labelled him as dyslexic.

Logically, the school should have helped him with his reading problems; instead, school authorities insisted that he needed an IQ test, although the provincial guidelines did *not* require one. The school authorities told his mother that they would not accept my report without an IQ test and she would have to pay a private psychologist to administer it. As a single mother and a student on a limited budget, she could not afford to do so. Considering his good scores on mathematics and visual-spatial tests and his superb computer skills, there was ample evidence that Jason was intelligent. Why would the school need an IQ test? Why couldn't they just help him? The school failed to provide remedial instruction for Jason, and the situation became much worse.

Not long after this, Jason's mother received a telephone call from the police, saying, "We have your son, Jason, at the police station, Ms. Edwards. We found him buying crystal meth in an alley downtown."

Ms. Edwards was crushed. She had no idea that her son was using drugs; she had only noticed that Jason seemed moody and depressed. She started to cry when he confessed to working as a prostitute to earn money to buy crystal meth.

Where did the road to crystal meth start? Ms. Edwards believes it started in grade 2 when Jason's reading problems were not recognized and when he did not receive any help for them. In the early grades, Jason was well behaved and popular, but the situation deteriorated with each passing year.

With the onset of adolescence, Jason became severely depressed, and his behaviour became anti-social and aggressive. He was extremely frustrated and angry with school, and often expressed his frustration with rage. He developed suicidal and paranoid behaviours. He ran away from home several times. He felt so rejected and ignored by the system that he gravitated to street youth and drug addicts. According to Jason, he turned to heavy drug use "because it is the only thing that makes me feel better!" In his mother's words, "A once very sweet child has become a monster."

The school system seemed immune to the depths of his despair. Never looking below the surface for why Jason was struggling in school, the school authorities saw only his "bad behaviour." Although he attended an alternative schooling program, it was geared more towards supporting students with behavioural difficulties than students with learning disabilities. Jason continued to search for relief through drugs, which resulted in more aggressive behaviour and poor judgement. In high school, he continued to see a school counsellor when he misbehaved, but he received no help for his reading.

Jason's mother described her son as follows:

> Jason was a kind and very sensitive person before his academic downfall in schools. He started school as a happy boy and in the initial years of school he was popular and well behaved. With the frustrations that he experienced in school because of his dyslexia, he was no longer that young boy. I had always hoped that with help, including rehab, he would be able to regain some of the strengths he

once had. He was very creative. I think he could have used these creative talents to make a future for himself as an artist or musician. However, he was often very negative about his abilities, probably because he had so much failure.[2]

Who can disagree with her when she said, with tears in her eyes and a catch in her voice, "The school district killed my son." Of course, the school administrators did not murder him with a gun or a knife. But they ignored his dyslexia, even though my assessment confirmed it. This callous treatment of a young student eventually led to Jason's death.

Lessons Learned

In most cases, learning disabilities persist throughout an individual's lifetime. The transition from the requirements in elementary school to demands in high school may place additional pressure on individuals with learning difficulties. For example, when they are required to read longer and more complicated texts that need a higher level of reading comprehension, and have more assignments that require extensive writing, adolescents with learning disabilities are at a great disadvantage. In addition, the emotional "storm and stress" that characterizes the adolescent years may also influence the performance of adolescents with learning disabilities.

Jason's case study is a true story about a student who was not identified as learning disabled in his childhood. During his adolescence, he was at greater risk for social, emotional, and academic failure. In fact, this case study illustrates several of the most critical questions in the field of learning disabilities, especially with regard to adolescents with learning disabilities.

Why did the school authorities not help Jason? Why did they not test him earlier? Why did they not accept my diagnosis of dyslexia? Why did they insist on an IQ test? Only the insensitive and bureaucratic individuals who made these decisions know the answers to these questions.

Unlike some of the case studies of successful people who had learning disabilities—those of Agatha Christie, William Butler Yeats, Greg Louganis, Hans Christian Andersen, and Winston Churchill—Jason's story has no happy ending. The school administrators did not light the match, but they were clearly a guilty partner in Jason's suicide.

22

The String Inside My Head
Struggles and Triumphs

Something inside my head stopped me from answering. It actually felt as though my skull housed a whole ball of string, with an end sticking out of my crown. I thought that if I pulled at this, I could get the string out, empty my head of it and unravel the tangle in my brain.

—Susan Hampshire

Susan Hampshire, the celebrated English actor, wrote these words in her memoir, *Susan's Story*, an account of her struggles and triumphs living with dyslexia. She is best known for her many television and film roles, including starring as the character Fleur in the BBC television series *The Forsyte Saga*, which originally aired in the late 1960s.

The string inside Susan's head represents her confusion with print. She saw letters and words as a jumbled image on the page, mixed up like the shapes in a kaleidoscope. Spelling hurt her brain, though not in a physical sense; her struggle to read and spell words created emotional turmoil. Through Susan's eyes, we gain more insight into the world of dyslexics and how they can overcome obstacles and use their talents to achieve success.

Reading and spelling were hurdles for Susan. She could not grasp the sounds of the letters in the English language. She describes how she had to read and reread sentences, sometimes missing words or reading them in the wrong order, and often failing to remember what she had just read.

Saved by the Hamster

Reading, spelling, and writing difficulties made school a torture for Susan, especially when she had to read out loud in front of the class. When her turn came to read out loud, she would take her pet hamster, Whiskatina, out of her pocket and place it on her desk and feed it some seeds. The students in the class would turn, fascinated by the little creature, and Susan would be saved from the terrifying fate of reading out loud.

Susan used other techniques to win approval from her classmates and to distract them from her learning difficulties. She brought Whiskatina's babies to school and used them as bribes, selling them on days when she had particularly difficult lessons.

Surviving in School

Not all Susan's attempts to get out of doing schoolwork involved her hamster. She was willing to do all sorts of jobs, such as sweeping the floor, clearing away the chairs, stacking the books, and putting away the art supplies, to win the approval of the teacher. She smiled and laughed a lot so that people would "forget she was stupid." Being charming and helpful was her way of coping in school. She made friends with the cleverest children in the class, bribing them so that she could copy homework from them in exchange for money, candy, and small toys.

Susan had trouble paying attention in school and avoided doing work that she found too difficult. She concentrated on everything other than her work, staring out of the window or at the lights on the ceiling instead of at the paper in front of her. She counted the minutes until recess or lunchtime. Her memories reminded me of when I asked a dyslexic nine-year-old what his favourite school subjects were. He quipped, with a straight face, "Recess," but hastily added, "I like lunch too."

Examinations were another hurdle for Susan. Faced with an examination in Latin, Susan complained that the type was too small and her eyes and head ached. The questions were incomprehensible to her, so she just doodled on the examination paper. Susan recalled that she was sure that the ball of string was filling her head from ear to ear.

Living with Dyslexia

Dyslexia affected every aspect of Susan's life. She dreaded getting mail because it required reading. She hated having to call anyone on the telephone because it meant looking up the number and remembering it long enough to dial it. She enjoyed cooking but could not read recipes. She could not help her son with his English homework, or read him bedtime stories, or complete an application for child allowance. Often cheques that she wrote were returned because the words and numbers did not match.

Her Acting Career

Susan chose a difficult career, that of an actor, but it was what she really wanted, and she pursued it with energy and determination. Although she eventually became a celebrated actor, it was a long and bumpy road to success. Because of her poor memory—a problem shared by many people with dyslexia—memorizing scripts was a struggle for her. She developed a strategy of reading the words over and over again in a quiet place, concentrating on the meaning of the lines to help her remember them. She says that it took her two to three times as long as the average actor to read a script and five to six times as long to learn her lines.

As an aspiring actor, Susan was required to audition for parts. It is usual for actors to get the script at the audition and read through the part immediately, with no rehearsal. Such "cold" reading was impossible for Susan, as she had no time to practise. Susan had a lovely singing voice and was a good dancer, so early in her career she chose singing auditions rather than ones that required reading lines. Many of her early roles were in musicals.

At the beginning of her career, a producer asked Susan to read a children's story on television. Terrified of reading, but needing the work, she felt nervous and physically ill. On the day of the recording her fear grew, and she was terrified at the thought of having to read in front of studio staff, camera crews, and millions of viewers. She wrote that her legs went numb and she dragged herself down the corridor. This was one of the times when she felt as if her head had turned into a ball of string. She was paralyzed with fear and almost fell on the floor because she could not see the chair.

On another occasion she took a job providing commentary for a fashion show, which again involved reading a prepared script. She welcomed everyone to the collection but called it "boring" instead of Braemar. She misread "V-neck sweater in blue" as "B deck sweat in Peru." She continued by saying this jumper has "tribbed ruffs" instead of "ribbed cuffs," and called it "sparky and tart" instead of "smart and sporty." These are the kind of errors that people with dyslexia often make. Sweating profusely and red in the face, Susan reluctantly crept up to the manager's office afterwards, waiting for the guillotine to fall. In fact, he interpreted her mistakes as clever quips and praised her entertaining performance.

Using Her Talents to Survive

Dyslexics learn differently than non-dyslexics. Susan used visual imagery and colour-coded her scripts to help her learn them. She learned her parts by trying hard to understand the character and the period and subject of the play.

Using her talents for singing, dancing, and acting helped Susan survive the awful times, the despair and the desperation caused by her dyslexia. Susan had "good days" when her brain seemed to be working and she understood the messages on the page. On these days she did not confuse letters or need to reread the print. Her eyes, ears, mouth, and brain were all working together.

Throughout Susan's account of her life with dyslexia, we can sense her struggle with her feelings of inferiority. She attended school at a time when dyslexia and other learning disabilities were not recognized. Not believing in her own worth, she sought praise and recognition from others. She believes that acting was a kind of therapy, a way of escaping from her failures, her low self-esteem, and the harshness of her life. The supportive environment of her home was immensely helpful, but the anguish created by her dyslexia has never left her. As a mature adult, she came to terms with it. Identifying her problem helped, as did the understanding of some skilled professionals. Yet the scars remain with her forever.

Being identified as dyslexic does not stop skeptics or solve all problems. A doubting teacher told Susan that she did not believe in dyslexia and that it was just laziness. This teacher said that Susan would not be able to act in plays like those of Tom Stoppard if she really had a problem.

Coming Out as Dyslexic

A chance remark led Susan to discover the truth about her disability. At an audition, one of the stagehands noticed how sad she looked and asked what was wrong. With tears in her eyes, she told him that she found reading at auditions impossible. The stagehand told her that he had a brother who was bright but had difficulty reading; his condition was called "word blindness" (the original name for dyslexia). Hearing this phrase changed Susan's life. She explains, "It gave me a 'hook' to hang my trouble on. It was a phrase I could use as a cover for the problem I couldn't understand." Like most people with dyslexia, Susan had spent almost her entire life trying to hide her reading problems.

Susan makes a strong case for diagnosing learning disabilities. She wanted to admit to the world that she was dyslexic, in part so that she could help other people with dyslexia, but she was frightened to speak publicly about it. When she acknowledged her dyslexia publicly, it did not hurt her career. In fact, several directors showed extraordinary sympathy and understanding. She was invited to participate in a BBC documentary and has received many invitations to speak about dyslexia. After the publication of her memoir in 1981, she went on to write numerous other books for adults and children, including books on her favourite hobby, gardening. She became a prominent campaigner in the UK on dyslexia issues and has raised money for research on dyslexia. In

1995, she was appointed an Officer of the Order of the British Empire in connection with her work.

In the next chapter, we will meet Greg Louganis, who also used acting to bolster his self-esteem and escape from what he thought were his failures.

23

Drowning, Diving, and Surfacing

*When I looked in the mirror, I saw an ugly kid who
had a hard time reading. I felt terribly isolated and
depressed, and was convinced that nobody could or
would want to understand me.*

—Greg Louganis

These are the words of elite athlete and Olympic gold medal
diver Greg Louganis, who achieved four gold medals and one
silver at the Olympics for his diving. In addition to his Olympic
triumphs, he won forty-seven US national diving titles and five
world championships in diving. He has been honoured by pres-
idents and has received accolades from the press and admiration from the public. Yet all of these accomplishments have not
erased the scars from the severe emotional turmoil Louganis
suffered while growing up.

In his autobiography, *Breaking the Surface*, co-written with Eric Marcus, Louganis tells the story of the powerful impact that dyslexia had on his life. He struggled with reading and other difficulties caused by dyslexia, often felt isolated, and battled low self-esteem and depression. Yet he discovered he had a great gift for acrobatics and diving and became one of the most accomplished divers of all time.

Early School Years

Greg was, in his mother's words, "a happy-go-lucky" child. He looked forward to starting school because he thought it would be like his acrobatics classes, and he was eager to learn. But starting in first grade, he had trouble with reading. For dyslexics like Greg, the words swim before their eyes and they feel like they are drowning in print. They cannot learn to read the way most people do. They are plagued with problems in spelling; even simple words are a problem. They read slowly, experience memory lapses, and have illegible handwriting that even they cannot read.

Greg says that he had to read a sentence over several times before he could understand its meaning. This is a common complaint among people with dyslexia; they struggle to read the words and then forget the beginning of the sentence before they come to the end of it.

Greg's aunt struggled to teach him but gave up in anger and disgust; his mother, although sympathetic, could not understand his reading problem. People attempting to teach people with dyslexia to read often experience similar frustrations. Dyslexia leaves parents and teachers and children puzzled.

When Greg was in school in the late 1960s and early 1970s, dyslexia was not generally recognized in schools. He believed that he was slow and stupid, and his teachers thought that he was lazy. His dyslexia was not diagnosed until he was in college. Greg's school years became a battleground between dyslexia and his self-esteem. His self-esteem lost.

To reduce their emotional pain, people with dyslexia often develop a pattern of trying to please their teachers, be helpful and obedient, and do everything they can to avoid being called on to read. Greg sat at the back of the classroom, volunteered to erase the blackboard, and did everything he could to be "the good little boy." Usually he succeeded in not getting called on by the teacher. You may recall from the previous chapter that Susan Hampshire used similar strategies to cover her dyslexia.

Greg was never comfortable expressing himself in words. Like many people with dyslexia, he used other means to communicate. In university, he benefited from learning in small groups. When that was not possible, Greg struggled in silence because he was ashamed to disclose his problem with reading, fearing others would consider him stupid. It is common for people with dyslexia to be ashamed to admit their difficulties for fear of being judged.

Greg writes in his autobiography that he was bullied because of his learning disability from the time he started school. Because of his stutter, he was put in a speech therapy class where most of the children were mentally delayed. He began to believe that he was mentally handicapped like the other children in the class.

Arithmetic Difficulties

Like many people with dyslexia, Greg had difficulty with numbers and calculations as well as with reading, writing, and spelling. Once he made a minor arithmetic error when he calculated the difficulty of a dive but, in this case, the error allowed him to qualify for the Olympics.

Self-Doubts and Depression

From childhood on, Greg had strong negative feelings about himself. He writes, "At first, I was one of the last ones picked for team sports because I was small, but once the other kids began to realize that I was athletically gifted, I was often chosen as team captain in volleyball, kickball, and softball. Despite my athletic abilities, there was always a part of me that wanted to hide, a part that felt inadequate. No matter how well I did, I'd look at the other kids and think, I wish I could be like everybody else."[1]

Greg was often critical of himself, had very little self-confidence, and felt like a failure. He writes, "When I looked in the mirror, I saw an ugly kid who had a hard time reading. I felt terribly isolated and depressed, and was convinced that nobody could or would want to understand me. I played negative messages over and over again in my head: My natural parents didn't want me; my adoptive parents don't love me; I'm retarded; I'm ugly."[2] These negative thoughts increased Greg's anger at himself and made him even more depressed.

As an adult looking back, Greg writes that he now recognizes that depression has been a major problem throughout his life and that he had signs of it while he was growing up.

Bullies and Victims

Part of the emotional trauma for people with dyslexia is the verbal abuse that they receive from other children. Greg's classmates teased and tormented him, calling him "retard" because he had trouble reading. Even when he changed schools, the label followed him. At the new school where he began fourth grade, there was not just name-calling; his classmates became violent. Some of the school bullies beat him up, demanded his lunch money, and accused him of bumping into them in the lunch line. When he refused to fight back, they called him "sissy-boy faggot."

Greg was ashamed of his failure to defy the bullies and kept his torment a secret. He did not want his mother to know what was going on, because he thought she might be ashamed of him. Hiding the experience of being bullied from parents and teachers is common because the victims of bullying are often afraid that they deserve the attacks.

Using convoluted logic that made sense to him at the time— and likely still makes sense to many struggling kids today— Greg writes in his autobiography, "I always thought that right prevailed, so since I got my butt kicked, I figured I must be wrong. They must be right to call me names and beat me up. Since I got beat up, I must be a bad person. Since I was a bad person, I must deserve it. If I didn't deserve it, I would have won the fights."[3]

"Sticks and stones will break my bones, but names will never hurt me" is a children's taunt often heard on playgrounds and schoolyards. Unfortunately, it is not true. Name-calling hurts and leaves lasting scars. Bullies hurt other children with words as well as fists. Children can be very cruel to each other; adults often do little to stop such cruelty.

Dan Olweus, a Norwegian psychologist who is recognized as a pioneer and a world-leading expert on research about bully/ victim problems among schoolchildren and youth, provides the following profile of bullies and their victims: Bullies pick on helpless, younger, and weaker students. The typical victims of bullies are sensitive and quiet and withdraw when attacked. They suffer from low self-esteem, have a negative view of themselves, and feel stupid, ashamed, and unattractive.[4] This description fits

Greg, the victim, perfectly. Greg was small and not aggressive, he withdrew when attacked, and he felt stupid, ugly, and ashamed.

The humiliation Greg experienced at the hands of his cruel schoolmates left deep emotional scars. It is a mistake to assume that children live in an innocent and happy world. The world can be full of turmoil and terror for many children, especially for those with dyslexia and other learning disabilities.

It is a tragedy that Greg had to endure so much pain. If his dyslexia had been identified, explained, and treated before the other children teased him and before his parents and teachers thought that he was just lazy and not concentrating on his schoolwork, much of his emotional pain could have been avoided.

Suicide Attempts

In his teenage years, life looked very bleak for Greg. When he was twelve, he grabbed some pills from his parents' medicine cabinet in a suicide attempt, but he did not take enough to cause damage. In high school, Greg attempted suicide again. He recalls, "I wrote a suicide note explaining that I couldn't take it anymore. I swallowed a handful of pills, got into bed, and prayed that I wouldn't wake up. When I opened my eyes the next morning and realized I was still alive, I was angry with myself for being such a failure that I couldn't even kill myself."[5]

The emotional stress and feelings of inadequacy that many adolescents with learning disabilities experience make them vulnerable to thoughts of suicide. We know from research that if adolescents do not get help for their learning problems, some succeed in ending their lives at a young age. Greg urges parents and teachers to pay attention to adolescent depression, look for its causes, and not ignore pleas for help.

Gymnastics, Dancing, and Diving

After his second suicide attempt, diving helped Greg to deal with his emotional turmoil. Diving helped develop his self-esteem; it was a type of therapy for him. A particularly sensitive coach helped Greg learn the difference between being a good sportsman and winning at the expense of integrity and fair play.

Greg's impressive talents for diving, acrobatics, and dancing helped him develop the inner strength and resources that saved him from drowning in total despair over his dyslexia. He writes, "Thank goodness for the acrobatics and the diving. Without them, I'm not sure how I would have gotten through what turned out to be a challenging and lonely childhood. Getting taunted and beaten up by kids at school, and fighting off my own terrible moods, there were times when I wanted to give up. But then I'd go to a talent contest and win first prize or do well in diving practice, and everything would be okay—for a while at least."[6]

Although people with dyslexia must continually confront difficulties stemming from their disability, they can overcome some of their problems by focusing on their abilities. Greg offers a good example of this. Since he was not very good at school, particularly in reading, he strove to excel in gymnastics and acrobatics. He writes, "This was one way to prove that I wasn't retarded. I may have brought home D's from school, but I could go out on stage and get applause and win first prize at competitions. I found the one thing I was good at, but being good at something wasn't enough—I had to be the best at it."[7]

Greg's words teach us an important lesson. We must help people with learning disabilities to identify and build on their strengths. Ask what they *can* do well. We must provide opportunities for the talent to be displayed and offer praise for acts well done. Dyslexics often have unusual talents in music, drama, art, sports, dancing, or mechanical skills. Greg showed an early interest in, and a talent for, gymnastics and acrobatics. By age nine, he had already performed many times on local talent shows and in convalescent homes.

Visual Thinking

Like many people with dyslexia, Greg was able to visualize images clearly in his head without looking at a picture. Before a dive in the 1988 Summer Olympics in Seoul, Korea, Greg went through the dive in his mind, visualizing each step and playing music in his head to the beat of the dive. He executed his dives with the words of the song "Believe in Yourself" from the musical *The Wiz* circulating over and over in his head.

He had an extraordinary ability to imagine movements in his head. He calls it his kinetic memory. When learning difficult new dives, he writes, "Before I did each one, 1 had to be able to visualize it, which meant that I had to see somebody else do it before I'd give it a try. When I visualized the dive in my head, it would take about three seconds to go through the dive, but I would see it in slow motion. I don't know how I did that, but because I could see it in slow motion, I was able to take the dive apart and memorize it step by step."[8] This kind of visual memory is a strength of some people with dyslexia and makes it possible for them to excel in the visual arts or sports or design or architecture.

Acting

Life was difficult for Greg, but acting was a type of therapy. He writes, "That's one of the reasons I fell in love with acting in the first place. You can be anyone you want and do anything you want."[9] He recalls identifying with a character called Darius, a role he played in a production of *Jeffrey*, by US playwright Paul M. Rudnick. Greg writes in his autobiography:

> I came to envy Darius as if he were a real person or a friend of mine. I admired his zest for life, which was something I was still struggling with. . . . Darius did a good job of enjoying life and conveying that joy to those around him. All of his down moments were offstage, which was exactly when I had to be up. Offstage I had to put on a happy face for the other cast members, because I didn't want anyone to know what was going on in my head. I had to "play" Greg the character, who is a lot happier than Greg the real person. At the time, I was lucky if I could just stay afloat and not get overwhelmed by my emotions.[10]

At college, Greg's talent for acting and dancing helped him find some success. When he participated in dramatic productions, he socialized with people in the way he could never do in school because of the teasing about his dyslexia. Recalling his role as assistant choreographer for a successful production of the Gilbert and Sullivan opera *The Gondoliers*, Greg says this success helped to build his self-confidence.

After the 1976 Summer Olympics, when he was sixteen, several people told Greg that he could work as an actor or in commercials. He was inspired by two elite Olympic athletes, Bruce Jenner, who went on to become a TV celebrity, and Mark Spitz, who worked in corporate endorsements after his swimming career. It was not difficult for Greg to perform in front of an audience—he had been doing that for years—but speaking in front of a crowd was a new challenge. When he took his first acting classes, he lacked confidence in his ability to communicate feelings and ideas.

Vulnerability

Because of his low self-esteem, even as an adult Greg was naive and anxious to please. This made him vulnerable to being victimized by people who took advantage of him. Various people extorted money from him, involved him in unwise investments, and cheated him out of money that was due to him. Other people, including a former lover, berated Greg for mistakes that are typically made by people with dyslexia.

When he won a silver medal in diving at the 1976 Summer Olympics, Greg was angry at himself for not winning gold. He thought that he was stupid and a failure at diving. When his coach yelled at him for rather insignificant mistakes, Greg blamed himself. Even when fans expressed admiration for him, Greg's lack of self-esteem prevented him from seeing himself in the positive light in which others saw him. When parents told him that they wished their children could be like him, his reaction was, "Would they feel that way if they *really* knew me? My second thought has always been I wouldn't wish my life on anyone."[11]

The outside world saw only the handsome, successful, and talented Greg. No one saw the vulnerable, unhappy Greg, embarrassed about his dyslexia. When we see only the glamour, the medals, and the adulation of the crowd, we fail to see the hard work, the long and circuitous road to victory, the injuries, the sleepless nights, and the charlatans who hover like vultures waiting to take financial advantage of their unsuspecting victims. There is often a high price for success, especially for vulnerable people such as Greg.

To gain what they think is the respect and friendship of others, children and adolescents with learning disabilities often have the misguided view that if they engage in anti-social behaviour of some kind, such as stealing or taking drugs, they will become "one of the crowd." They think that others will forget their dyslexia and stop calling them "retard" and they will become heroes in the eyes of their peers. Greg turned to drugs to try to get the respect of his schoolmates. He smoked marijuana to be accepted as part of the group.

The Next Chapter

Greg's story has a happy ending. He has acted in numerous films, been a guest on *The Oprah Winfrey Show*, worked as a diving coach, and been a mentor to the US diving team at the 2012 Summer Olympics in London. He also became a breeder and trainer of Harlequin Great Danes and has co-written, with Betsy Sikora Siino, a guide to dog ownership, *For the Life of Your Dog*.

For Greg, coming to terms with his dyslexia involved much anguish and hard work. Life would have been much easier for him if his dyslexia had been identified and treated when he was young. It is too late to erase the years of pain for Greg, but his success has helped him overcome some of the turmoil and self-loathing.

Greg's story teaches us an important lesson. We must identify children with learning disabilities early, before they experience the stress of failure, before they begin to hate themselves and think of suicide, and before other children tease and torment them. We also must help children without learning problems to understand more about what it is to experience difficulties in reading, writing, spelling, and arithmetic, and we must encourage the development of empathy. Even today, there are many children like Greg in schools, children who are sinking in a sea of incomprehensible words and sentences. We need to keep their heads above water by identifying and helping the children who are struggling in school. Allowing their gifts and talents to surface will benefit not only them but also their families and society as a whole.

The Chicken and the Egg

Greg was "a happy-go-lucky" child when he started school. As he became aware of his reading difficulties, his emotional problems began and got worse over time. Neither he, his parents, nor his teachers knew he was dyslexic. He felt stupid; his classmates called him "retard." His dyslexia was perhaps the most important cause of his emotional problems. Later he struggled with his sexual identity and came out as a homosexual. Of course, societal attitudes towards homosexuality can create emotional turmoil, but Greg's psychological difficulties started when he was a young child who experienced problems in school. The school troubles occurred well before his sexuality was an issue.

It is clear that if Greg's dyslexia had been recognized early in his school career and if he had received help for it, his emotional life and feelings about himself might have been quite different.

PART IV

Solutions

24

Teaching Basic Skills

Kyle, six years and six months old, was very proud that he had learned to read. He wanted to share this skill with his special friend, his cocker spaniel, Max, and decided that he would teach Max to read. "Max!" he said eagerly, "I am going to teach you to read!"

He showed Max one of his favourite storybooks and read the first sentence to Max. He then read a few words from the next sentence and said, "Now, Max, you read the rest." Max looked at him with his big brown eyes but did not say anything; instead, he wagged his tail.

Kyle thought to himself, "I bet the book is too hard for him. I'll get a simple book." He took a book that belonged to his little sister, Emma. There was only one word and a big picture on each page. He showed the book to Max and said, "Look, Max, see apple," pointing to the word *apple* under a picture of an apple. Max sniffed the page. Kyle said, "This word says *apple*. Okay, Max, what does this word say?" Max licked Kyle's hand but did not reply.

Kyle thought, "First I should teach him the letters." He grabbed two plastic letters from the door of the refrigerator and showed Max the red A and the yellow B. He said, "Max, pay attention." Very slowly and deliberately, he said to Max, "This is an *A*"—holding it in his right hand for the dog to see—"and this is a *B*"—holding it in his left hand. Max looked at him quizzically. Kyle mixed up the two letters in his hand, threw them on the floor, and said, "Max, which one is *A*?" Max wagged his tail and looked at him. Kyle picked up the letters again, mixed them up, and threw them down on the floor. "Which is *B*?" Max licked them both. Kyle tried hard but Max could not learn.

"Max, why can't you learn?" Kyle said. Then he turned to Max and said, "You must be dyslexic. We'll have to take you to Dr. Siegel to be tested." Fortunately, Kyle did not choose a cat or a goldfish, or he would have been even more frustrated.

Kyle is a real little boy whose identity has been changed to protect him. His aunt was a student working in a clinic where children were tested for learning disabilities. Kyle was very eager to share his newly acquired teaching skill. His heart was in the right place, but his methods were a bit primitive. His pupil was enthusiastic but not capable of learning to read. Our methods for teaching reading to people with dyslexia are a little more sophisticated.

Reading and Phonics

Helping people with learning disabilities begins with good teaching of the basic skills. People learning to read in English or any alphabetic language need to be taught the sound of the letters (phonics). Of course, that is not all that they need to be taught, but they do need to learn it. Dyslexic children struggle with the sounds of letters. Here are some of their observations:

"The alphabet would be a lot easier if there were not so many letters in it."

"I don't do _w_'s," said one boy when I asked him to read the word _how_. Admittedly _w_ is a hard letter.

"How do you expect me the read them if they are not words," said one nine-year-old girl when I asked her to read some non-words. She was accustomed to memorizing words, not sounding them out, because she lacked the basic skills necessary for decoding words that she had not seen before or memorized.

People with dyslexia need systematic instruction in phonics. For years, there has been a controversy, called the "reading wars," about how to teach reading. One group advocates phonics—that is, learning the sounds of the letters. Another group advocates a philosophy called "whole language." Whole-language philosophy revolves around the idea that one does not teach word analysis out of context. In other words, you do not analyze individual words; you guess the meaning of words based on the context provided by the sentence. If you take this position to extremes, when you reach a stop sign you refuse to read it because it is not in a sentence. Once when I explained how you can use the errors that children make to understand how they process information, a whole-language proponent informed me, "We do not read words out of context." I was tempted to ask if this was the eleventh commandment.

The reading war can get nasty. Whole-language advocates accuse the phonics supporters of ignoring the role of meaning in reading and instead drilling the children on letter-sound relationships and nothing else. This is nonsense. Teachers who teach phonics also teach many other aspects of reading. Readers of this book may wonder why anyone would argue about phonics. Why not teach both phonics and meaning-related skills, as most good reading teachers do?

There are a number of good programs to teach phonics and other reading-related skills to dyslexic children. These programs include Orton-Gillingham (www.orton-gillingham.com), Lindamood-Bell (www.lindamoodbell.com), and the Wilson program (www.wilsonlanguage.com). These programs are designed for teachers and tutors, and using them requires training. There are programs available online that can help teach children reading and writing skills; one of these programs is ABRACADABRA (abralite.concordia.ca). It helps children learn phonological awareness, phonics, reading fluency, and reading comprehension skills. The web version is a short version of the program; the long version is available to schools and other institutions. Both versions are free of charge. Another program, called ePEARL (grover.concordia.ca/epearl/), teaches reading comprehension and writing skills. There are also some helpful books that explain reading and ways to help children with reading difficulties.[1]

Some educators are not certain how to help students with dyslexia. They seem reluctant to recognize struggling readers in their classrooms and appear not to recognize that good classroom instruction is necessary. Some believe that if they encounter a child who is a struggling reader, rather than trying to help the child in the classroom, the solution is to send the child to a special education teacher. Science fiction giants Larry Niven and Jerry Pournelle propose a different fate for teachers who do not help children with reading problems. In their book *Inferno*, the character Mrs. Herrnstein did not help children with reading problems (she thought that they were not smart), so she was turned into a monster in hell with her head on backwards so her tears ran between her buttocks.

Vocabulary

There is more to reading than learning the sounds of the letters. After the age of six, we learn most of our new vocabulary from reading. Children with reading problems do not like to read, so they spend much less time reading than good readers. As a result, they do not develop vocabulary at the same pace. One student remarked, "I would rather clean the toilets than read." One solution is to read aloud to them, as this helps develop their ear for language and improves their vocabulary. Learning prefixes and suffixes (for example, *dis-*, as in *disapprove* and *disappear*, or *-ology*, as in *anthropology* and *sociology*) also helps build vocabulary.

Rick Riordan has written a series of books for children in which the central character, a boy named Percy Jackson, has dyslexia and an attention deficit.[2] I recommend these books for children with learning disabilities. The mystery writer Anne Perry also has written four books about a dyslexic girl who goes back in history.[3] They are especially designed to appeal to girls with dyslexia. I also recommend consulting the website Lovereading4kids (www.lovereading4kids), which lists dyslexia-friendly books for various age ranges.[4]

Grammar

People with dyslexia often have problems with grammar; not necessarily major problems, but subtle ones. For example, dyslexics are not as proficient as good readers in predicting the missing word in a sentence that is read to them. For example, try predicting the missing words in these two sentences: "The girl _____ is tall plays basketball well." "_____ is Susan going to the doctor today?" In the first sentence, the correct answer is "who." Many children at age eleven or twelve can answer this correctly. Children (and even some adults) with dyslexia find this sentence difficult because of the complex construction. They usually say the missing word is "she." In the second sentence, "when" or "why" is correct (or even "how"). Although many children at age eleven or twelve can answer this correctly, children with dyslexia are confused and often cannot think of anything to say. These difficulties indicate some problems with working memory—that is, remembering the sentence for long enough to be able to answer it.

Spelling

Teaching spelling to dyslexics in any language is difficult. Spelling in any alphabetic language involves both phonological processing—that is, understanding how sounds in the language translate into letters—and visual memory—that is, remembering what words look like, because many words cannot be spelled just by the sound of the letters. English spelling is not entirely predictable, as you see when you consider words like *should*, *thought, thorough, rough, cow,* and *low.*

The first step in teaching spelling is, of course, teaching how sounds are represented in English. However, that is not enough. Using this system, one could spell *education* as *educashun* or *said* as *sed* or *walked* as *walkd.*

Dyslexic children have trouble remembering the order of sounds within a word when they want to spell. The following is a true story a parent told me.

Ellen stared at the badges arranged in neat rows on the table. She went to the *R*s to find hers. It was "Meet the Teacher" night and all the parents were coming to the school. They were all supposed to get name tags. She saw one with the name "Mrs. Rosenderp."

"What a strange name," she thought. "I've never seen anything like it. I wonder what kind of name it is." She thought that perhaps in was a Dutch name. Ellen hoped that the woman with this strange name would come to pick up her name tag so she could meet her. She had to meet her son Mark's teacher at 7:15 p.m., so she had to hurry to find her name tag and go to the classroom. Five minutes before her appointment, she panicked: Where was her name tag?

"Oh no," she cried. The people clustered at the table stared at her. There was no tag with the name "Rosenberg." Then she realized that her dyslexic son had trouble spelling his own name.

There are many aspects to learning spelling apart from learning vocabulary. Another aspect is learning the meaning and spelling of common prefixes and suffixes in English, such as *pre-*, *tri-*, and *-ful*. In English, the endings of many words are clues to their meaning. For example, endings such as *-ness*, *-sion*, *-tion*, *-ity*, *-ist*, and *-ism* usually indicate a noun; the endings *-ive*, *-able*, *-ful*, *-al*, and *-ous* usually indicate an adjective; *-ly* usually signifies an adverb; and *-ize* and *-ify* usually indicate a verb. If people with learning disabilities learn these endings and what they signify, their spelling will improve.

One of the confusing aspects of the English language for poor spellers is when to use double consonants in the middle of a word. Here is a rule that works most of the time: If the vowel preceding the consonant is long (stressed), the consonant does not get doubled; for example, *later, miner, minor, litre,* and *biter.* If the vowel preceding the consonant is short (not stressed), the consonant is doubled: for example, *better, manner, bitter, mitten, litter, little,* and *kitten.* Similar rules apply to multi-syllabic words, with some exceptions. Remembering these rules may help poor spellers.

Imagine that you had to decide which of the non-words *filv* or *filk* could be a word. The correct answer is *filk* because no English word ends in *v*. Surprisingly, dyslexics were better at this task than good readers. People with dyslexia have poor phonological skills so they learn to pay more attention to what words look like. Good readers can rely on their phonological skills so they pay less attention to what words look like and are more likely to accept a word on the basis of sound.

Mathematics

Although calculators can help children with mathematical calculations, children still have to be taught the underlying logic of mathematics. John Mighton, a mathematician, has developed one promising program, called JUMP Math.[5] It systematically breaks mathematical concepts into small units in logical sequences and then teaches generalization to larger numbers.

Parents can help children with mathematics by playing games that involve counting and numbers, and by helping children learn how to make change and letting children manage their allowance. In my family we played a game called Licence Plate Bingo on long car rides. First everyone in the car looked for licence plates with the number 1, then 2, then 3, and so on, as high as we could go. If you are looking for 31, you need to find a licence plate with a 3 and a 1 in any order. When you find the number, you yell, "31 bingo!" We once got as high as 78, but that was long car ride.

Memory

"I am not a slow learner; I am a fast forgetter," remarked one eleven-year-old girl who was having reading and spelling problems. Children with learning difficulties often have trouble remembering the order of letters in a word, along with many other memory problems.

In a grade 4 class that I taught, students read a book and were asked to make a booklet summarizing and illustrating the story. A dyslexic girl in the class titled her booklet *The Wizard of Zo*. Another student said, "We had to learn the times tables, which I learned and forgot every day."

Memory problems are difficult to overcome. However, logical reasoning may be an alternative. I have a friend who can't remember multiplication tables—I talk about her in the next chapter. When I asked her what 7×9 was, she said that she multiplies 7×10 and then subtracts 7.

Understanding basic concepts may help with memory. Visualizing may also help; for example, visualizing the items that you need to buy in the supermarket may help you remember them.

Writing

One of the most important lessons that children need to learn about writing is to take the role of the reader. Making sure that readers understand what you are writing is critical. Practising writing and getting feedback are an excellent way to develop writing skills. Computers are important aids for people whose handwriting is messy and laborious.

Solutions

Teachers, tutors, and parents need to look beyond the errors that children make, looking for the reasons behind the errors. But a word of caution is in order. It can be very stressful and frustrating for parents to try to help their own children with learning disabilities. Doing so may disrupt the parent-child relationship. Schools need to take responsibility for providing remedial help to all children. I urge parents to advocate on behalf of their children to get the help they need.

25

Technology and Other Ways of Helping People with Learning Disabilities

Imagine being able to talk to your computer and watch it type what you say. This scenario is not the invention of a science fiction writer. There is software called "speech recognition" that allows you to talk into a microphone connected to the computer and what you say appears on the computer screen as if by magic. When I first used speech recognition software, I thought that there must be a little person inside the computer typing what I said. Initially the program was slow and made many mistakes; it took many hours to train it to recognize the user's voice. Now such programs are very efficient, and you can talk at your normal speed.

Obviously, speech recognition software is very helpful for people with learning disabilities, especially those with writing problems. Many other people can benefit from it too, including people for whom typing is difficult.

The user does have to learn to use the software. The program sometimes makes "silly" mistakes; if they are not corrected immediately, they will keep reoccuring over and over again. The program works on the basis of sound, not grammar, so it cannot tell the difference between *for* and *four* or *there*, *their*, and *they're*, or even *two* and *to* and *too*. When the software makes a mistake, you use a pull-down menu to correct a word or phrase.

Speech recognition software is only one of many compensatory techniques that can help people with learning disabilities. Compensatory techniques are strategies that are used when direct remediation may not be feasible or effective. Such compensatory techniques or accommodations offer people with learning disabilities ways to cope with difficulties in reading, writing, spelling, or mathematics. They are different than direct remedial intervention, or remedial strategies, which are attempts to directly treat the problems and try to eliminate the source of the difficulty (see chapter 24).

Other Accommodations Using Computers

Computers are essential for people who have writing problems, especially if their handwriting is illegible, and they should be provided by the schools. People who struggle with writing often say that they have trouble remembering how to form the letters; they cannot think and write at the same time. Typing, and especially word processing, is very useful for these people because the fine motor coordination used in typing is much simpler than the skills involved in handwriting.

In one study, we found that children who had access to computers showed improvement in the quality and quantity of their writing.[1] They enjoyed writing on the computer more than writing by hand. Writing an examination on a computer can also be quite helpful for those who struggle with handwriting.

Computer software enables people to check for spelling mistakes. The computer highlights words not found in its dictionary and suggests several alternative spellings. This software can be helpful for individuals with poor spelling skills; however, if you cannot spell well, it can be difficult to know which alternative spelling is correct. Suppose you meant to spell *nature* and you typed *natur*. The software would give you the choice of *nature* or *natural*. If you had been taught that *al* is often an adjectival ending and *ure* is often the ending of a noun, you could use grammar logic to help you choose the correct spelling.

Suppose you type the word *nachure*. The spelling software would give you a choice of *nacre*, *hachures*, *hachure*, *anchored*, and *nature*. You would probably know that the word starts with an *n* sound because even poor spellers usually recognize which letter represents the beginning sound in a word. So that would leave a choice between *nacre* and *nature*. You may have been taught that very few English words end in *cre* but many more end in *ure*, so using logic and some knowledge of the structure of words in the English language, you could choose the correct spelling. Poor spellers need to be taught such strategies to approach spelling.

Talking Books

Obviously, people with a reading disability experience a great deal of difficulty when they attempt to read. One compensatory technique is to provide audiobooks along with print books. In that way, the reader can follow the print and hear the words at the same time. This strategy helps build reading speed and vocabulary. Some people can remember what they hear much better than what they read, so listening to audiobooks can also be quite effective for memory problems. Screen readers are another type of accommodation for people with reading problems. These software programs read out loud what is on a computer screen. With some software, you can click on a word or phrase and the computer will read it to you.

Developing Interests

One of the most effective ways of teaching people with severe reading problems to read is by giving them books or magazines about topics that interest them. One of my students worked with a sixteen-year-old who was severely dyslexic and could barely read and spell. Understandably, he hated reading, but he was really interested in mountain bikes. He learned to read by poring over magazines about mountain biking. His interest overcame his distaste for reading. Now this young man is able to read road signs, prescription instructions, and labels in supermarkets, among other printed materials.

Another technique to help people with reading disabilities is to provide what are called high interest, low vocabulary books. These books stimulate interest in reading because the topics are of interest, but they are less frustrating for challenged readers than regular books because the vocabulary is deliberately simpler.

Rosalie Fink, an educator from Lesley University in Cambridge, Massachusetts, writes about successful people with dyslexia who were very late in developing reading skills.[2] The successful dyslexics she interviewed, including a Nobel laureate and other professionals in fields requiring extensive reading, such as law, medicine, business, and psychology, learned to read by reading books and magazines about subjects that interested them. They had a passionate interest in a particular subject and read widely in that subject, even though they read slowly. They developed an understanding of the terminology and the basic underlying concepts and used this knowledge as a technique to increase their decoding skills. They relied on context to guess new words.

These adults still have trouble sounding new words, have difficulty with spelling and handwriting, and experience other common difficulties associated with dyslexia, but they have achieved success and fulfillment in careers based on their passions. They all recommended capitalizing on a dyslexic person's interests to develop his or her reading skills. This approach to reading is sometimes referred to as "reading to learn."

Voice Recording Devices

Audio recorders are especially useful for children whose handwriting and typing skills are not well developed, as they allow the teacher to hear the quality of a child's ideas. I tested one eleven-year-old boy who was asked to write a composition about a picture showing some spacemen getting out of a spaceship and landing on a moon-like surface. He wrote four badly printed lines and spelled almost every word except "the" incorrectly. For example, he spelled *planet* as *plent* and *spaceship* as *speceshap*. If you looked at his story (which was hard to read because of the messy handwriting and the inaccurate spelling), you might think that it was not very creative. I then asked this boy to tell me a story about the picture, and I recorded it. When transcribed, the story was three single-spaced pages long, had a major plot and subplots, plus sound effects. The boy even made up a Martian language. By using an audio recorder, I was able to see how creative he was.

Calculators

Calculators are useful for people who have difficulty with number facts, multiplication tables, and memory. Everyone needs to learn estimation and problem-solving skills, because a calculator will not tell you what numbers to calculate, but the actual calculation can be done electronically. I am often asked, "How can a person succeed in mathematics without knowing the multiplication tables or number facts? Isn't a calculator just a crutch?" I relate the example of a friend who is a very successful mathematician, a distinguished professor at a Canadian university. She does not know her multiplication tables. If you ask her what 7×9 is, she takes out her calculator. If she does not have a calculator handy, or if the batteries are dead, she has a way of solving the problem that demonstrates her understanding of the concept of numbers. She related the following strategy: "I multiply 7×10 and take away 7." Obviously, she understands conceptually about multiplication, but she cannot remember the basic number facts. Conceptual understanding is the basis of mathematical thinking, but calculators can certainly be used for solving problems.

Suppose that a student has to solve the following problem: Which is a better buy, 5 cans of soup at $2.69 or 1 can at $0.56? The student needs to understand that one way to solve the problem is to divide 269 by 5 to determine how much one can costs. Alternatively, you can multiply $0.56 by 5 to calculate what 5 cans cost. Although these calculations may seem simple, they are difficult for some people. Using a calculator would help students who understand the concept but have a problem doing the calculation.

Other Coping Strategies

Individuals with a learning disability often develop some effective strategies for coping with their particular disability. The following are some examples of compensatory strategies people have told me about. One woman who could not remember how to spell out numbers and, therefore, had difficulty writing cheques, developed an ingenious system: she typed all the words for the numbers, reduced the size of the list on a photocopier, and attached it to her chequebook for quick reference.

One student tried to listen carefully and memorize as much as possible in lectures; he used the memorized phrases when he wrote essays. Another student reported that he used visual images to help his memory; in other words, he visualized what he heard as a tool to help with memory. One young woman with reading problems reported that as a child she listened very carefully when the teacher read a story and concentrated on memorizing it. When she was called on to read, she would read out loud from memory.

I remember giving a reading test to one seven-year-old boy. When I told his teacher he could barely read any of the words on the test, she was surprised at my findings because she thought he could read very well. She gave me his reader to show me and I took him aside. He read the first story without a single mistake. He read the second story and missed only a few words. He read the third story perfectly, but it was not the story that went with the picture on the page. He had memorized the stories but had forgotten which story went with which picture, and mistakenly recited the fourth story in the book. This boy developed a clever strategy, had a good memory, and was able to fool his teacher, but he still had a reading problem. His reading strategy was successful in the short run but was not, obviously, a permanent solution.

Not all strategies for coping with learning disabilities are appropriate, but they are born out of desperation. Some students count on schoolmates to whisper the answer to them when they are called on. Sometimes students break their non-existent glasses or lose them so that someone will read test questions to them. Students have been known to ask someone close by to drop their spelling paper on the floor so that they can see the correct spelling.

Techniques That Help Students in the Classroom

There are various techniques to help students with learning disabilities in the classroom. Sitting near the front of the classroom helps with concentration and attention; it is also harder for students to nod off in the front row. Copying from the board is a challenge for many students; being given photocopies of notes or presentation slides is very helpful. Taking notes during lectures and discussions is also difficult for many students, especially if they have writing problems. Some students prefer to use a computer to take notes. Others audio-record lectures so they do not miss important information while they are attempting to take notes.

It is very helpful for students with learning disabilities if teachers are patient and allow extra time for completing work. People with dyslexia need extra time to use compensatory strategies. As one student argued, "I have to take twice as long to do my reading." Having extra time to write essays is also important for students with writing difficulties.

When writing is a problem, students really appreciate feedback and help with organizing their essays. They need guidelines about forming and expressing their ideas. *Graphic organizers* are visual devices such as lines, boxes, and circles to organize information. They can help in structuring a composition or understanding a reading passage. Using a *semantic map*—a schematic version of the information organized into major concepts and subordinate concepts relevant to a topic—can help students with learning disabilities.

Examinations

Many students with learning disabilities think that having extra time for examinations helps them because they read or write more slowly than average students. However, this accommodation can be controversial because some people consider it unfair for some students to have extra time and not others. To test this idea, we conducted a study where we gave students extra time on a reading test. They took one test in twenty minutes, the standard amount of time, and then took an alternative but similar test and were given as much time as they needed. The dyslexic students had much higher scores when they had extra time, but the people without dyslexia had the same scores whether they had extra time or not. In fact, some of the non-dyslexic readers had lower scores with extra time. Possibly they thought too hard about the questions and looked for tricks in the questions. So some people may, in fact, do worse with extra time.

If we really want to test students' knowledge, not how fast they can think and write, perhaps we should give them as much time as they want on examinations.

Improvement But No Cure

It sounds pessimistic to say that there can be an improvement but no permanent cure for a learning disability. This reality can be hard to face. Unfortunately, the learning problems do not disappear with success in other areas. However, as Rosalie Fink's research has shown, if people with dyslexia are encouraged to pursue courses and careers that tap into all of their talents and interests, they may achieve satisfying careers.

26

The Great Cover-Up
What Parents Should Know to Avoid Being Victims of the System

Farmer Bill's barn catches fire. Fortunately, all of the animals escape unharmed. Due to the circumstances, the animals are all jumping and running around. In time, the fire department arrives. Now the question is what should they do first? If we believe what all the educators tell us, we must first settle down the animals. Of course, this makes little sense. The fact is we need to put out the fire. Once the fire has been extinguished then the animals will settle down in time.

—Don Reist

This wise parable by Don Reist, a teacher and special education specialist in Ajax, Ontario, makes an important point. He wants to warn parents about the "Great Cover-Up." Educators often see only a student's bad behaviour, not the underlying cause, which is often a learning disability that has not been properly identified or treated. Thus, the student acts out. Teachers believe that they should treat the behaviour problem but, in reality, learning disabilities are hiding behind behavioural problems. School personnel tell parents that their child's behaviour is the problem, failing to recognize the learning difficulties.

Teachers write on report cards, "Jessica cannot control her behaviour." "Kyle is disobedient and rude." "Alex does not pay attention and is off in a dream world." But they miss the fact that the child is struggling with reading, spelling, mathematics, and/or writing, leading to problems with self-esteem, lack of attention, and the desire to get noticed by other students, which is often achieved by acting out.

As Don Reist writes, "It always astounds me that many students with special needs are identified with a behaviour problem rather than a learning problem. . . . I am told, in no uncertain terms, that they [the teachers] cannot work with the learning problem until they have resolved the student's behaviour problem."[1] Those of us who work in the field realize that this idea of treating the behavioural problems without trying to find the cause of the behavioural problems is nonsense.

Don eloquently describes the anguish of students with learning disabilities: "Ask yourself this: Have you ever known a student who struggles in school? Have you sensed the pain on their face? The fact is the pain is quite real. There is nothing that I can think of more frustrating for a child than to fall behind in school. As the frustration grows, the child will start acting out this frustration. For most children it is preferable to be known as the class clown than for his peers to realize that he is falling behind." Dealing with behavioural problems is important, but it should not replace helping the child with learning difficulties in reading, spelling, writing, or mathematics.

The education system often misses some very important reasons for the behavioural problems. Rena Slabich, a former teacher and special education advocate in California, describes some situations that she has encountered in talking to students with learning disabilities. "I didn't realize he was behaving so terribly in math because he was so hungry as a result of being bullied at lunch!" and "I didn't realize she was refusing to do her work because she was supposed to be wearing glasses!"[2]

Dr. Susan Blumberg, a clinical psychologist in California, writes, "I did want to add that a frequent referring situation is when a child is not turning in homework, or not sitting still, or unable to focus on a long task, and then the school labels that child a troublemaker, and starts with disciplinary action, which, of course, makes things worse. As an advocate and psychologist, I then hear from parents about the behavior and we have to start from the beginning to assess the child's actual learning needs. . . . I look at behavior as the child's communication: frustration, avoidance behavior, etc., tells the story of something much greater that is going on."[3]

Schools sometimes blame parents, claiming they are anxious and overprotective. Or they blame the child: "she does not pay attention" or "he is anxious."

Dr. Patricia McGuire, a developmental and behavioural pediatrician in Cedar Rapids, Iowa, sums up the problem and proposes a solution: "I completely agree with the problem of thinking that the child's behavior has to be settled before learning can occur. If more people understood how to assess the 'whys' of the behavior, the more they would find out that frustration, confusion, and anxiety over not understanding or being able to demonstrate information is the source of the behavior. Help[ing] the student in these areas will magically cause the behaviors to resolve over time."[4]

The Great Cover-Up

Parents should not become victims of the school system. If they notice that their child is having a problem with reading, writing, spelling, and/or mathematics, they face a dilemma. What can they do?

The first step is to go to the school and try to discuss the problem with the teacher and the principal. If school personnel agree, this is a good sign. But parents must be prepared for such a meeting. They should take notes and get the names of all the personnel present. Often the child's mother assumes responsibility for attending such school meetings; however, if the child's father or uncle or an adult male friend accompanies the mother, she will likely get more respect. This situation is sad, and not true in all cases, but it occurs frequently. When I suggested to one mother that she bring her husband along to the meeting at the school where her eight-year-old son was having a great deal of trouble learning to read, she looked puzzled. Then her face lit up. She said, "He is six feet four inches tall and weighs 250 pounds." I was tempted to ask her if other families could borrow him for their meetings with school personnel.

What parents find at the school is not always a warm welcome. The teacher may say that the child is not really behind and just needs some time to catch up. This idea is nonsense. If a child is still struggling with beginning reading in the latter part of grade 1, then the child needs help.

The school principal may say that the school cannot help the child without first having psychoeducational testing done. However, as mentioned earlier, the child may have to wait up to two years for the testing. The parents may be told that they can get a private assessment, but it may cost as much as $2,500.

The solution is for the teacher or another staff person to do the testing that I discussed in chapter 11.

A particularly insidious trend is for schools to insist that a child who is struggling with reading, spelling, mathematics, and/or writing repeat a year. Parents should resist this suggestion of grade retention—that is, requiring a child to repeat a year. We know that retention hurts a child's self-esteem and does not provide the extra help that a child needs. The solution is not repeating a grade but providing remedial help for the child who is struggling.

Parents should demand what is called an Individual Education Plan (IEP). This is a plan that outlines the child's abilities and problems and provides a detailed program to help the child. The IEP, sometimes known by a slightly different name, specifies the educational goals for that child during the school year. It should provide details about what help the child will receive and who will provide the assistance (the classroom teacher or the remedial teacher or a specialist). Usually schools discuss the IEP with the parents and the parents sign it as a contract.

Navigating the maze of school bureaucracy can be frustrating and sometimes humiliating for parents. Kathryn Burke's book about her attempt to advocate for her child, titled *The Accidental Advocate*, provides many helpful hints and much encouragement. I highly recommend it.

Snake Oil for Sale

Having a child with a learning disability is often very frustrating and creates anxiety in parents. Parents and educators are often desperate for techniques to help children. They are faced with a bewildering array of methods that may or may not provide help. They search for a miracle cure. They would do well to remember that a magic pill for learning disabilities does not exist. The treatment road is littered with charlatans who promise the world and merely empty the pockets of unsuspecting consumers. Unscrupulous individuals attempt to sell "miracle cures" to parents of children with learning disabilities and to adults who have a learning disability. These miracle cures have not been scientifically proven to be effective.

Spotting the Snake Oil

Here are some ways to recognize deceptive practices:

- They promise a "cure" for learning disabilities. There is no permanent cure for a learning disability. There can be improvement but it takes time and some signs will remain.

- They claim that the scientific establishment has manufactured a conspiracy against them. All people in the learning disability field would welcome a cure if there is good evidence about its effectiveness.

- They claim that their technique changes the brain. They evoke brain plasticity as a new and revolutionary concept. Their technique is supposedly unique in that it can target certain areas of the brain and create changes that no other technique has achieved. It should be obvious that all learning changes the brain; no technique has a monopoly on this. For centuries educators have recognized that the brain is the centre of learning and change. The brain obviously changes as it learns; learning does not take place in the left elbow or the right big toe. The brain is extremely complex. It is a network of interconnected areas and nerve tracts; most functions, such a reading or doing mathematics, are not localized in one specific area.

- In the absence of scientific evidence, they claim that the program is valid because "many" schools use it. This rationale is not a reason to use a program.

- The proponents of the program use case histories and testimonials as the only evidence of the effectiveness of the program. Case histories cannot be replicated and are of limited value in judging effectiveness. Testimonials are not scientific evidence; it is impossible to evaluate the source. Any test of the effectiveness of a program must include a control group that does not get the treatment. Without a control group to measure against, any improvement could be caused by other factors, such as the development of the child, progress over time that would have happened without the intervention, and/or help from a good teacher or tutor independent of the program. Sometimes the participants in a program do not have a serious learning disability, so any improvement they show cannot be generalized to people with learning disabilities.

Parents and teachers should look for independent research published in refereed journals that shows the effectiveness of an intervention program. They should ask whether the program teaches basic skills in reading (or spelling, writing, mathematics). A US government website, What Works Clearinghouse, is a reliable source for information about the effectiveness of various programs; see ies.ed.gov/ncee/wwc/.

Tactics in the War for Hearts and Pocketbooks

In the war for consumer dollars, no technique is too shabby. A favourite technique is to threaten to sue people who are critical of a particular treatment method. When I pointed out that a treatment for learning disabilities called the Arrowsmith Program, described on its website as "a cognitive program for students with learning disabilities," had no empirical basis to support its claims, I received a letter from a Toronto law firm with the following statement: "My clients reserve their right to exercise all available legal remedies against you to protect their reputation and goodwill including an action against you for aggravated, actual and general damages for libel and slander."[5] There is no research published in peer-reviewed journals that supports this program.[6]

On hearing about the threatened suit, one blogger wrote, "Instead of spending money on expensive lawyers, why don't they spend it on research."

Colleagues in England have received similar threats from the developers of the Dore Programme, which describes itself as "a drug-free practical exercise programme that helps people tackle the root cause of learning difficulties."[7] These investigators noted that there was no research to support the claims.[8] Eventually the program went bankrupt.

Buyer Beware

The road to the pot of gold at the end of the rainbow is littered with magic cures for learning disabilities that do not work: vitamin C, sunflower seeds, an additive-free diet, or pills to relieve motion sickness. The older cures—sitting in a dark closet, standing in the back of the classroom with a dunce cap on your head, being whipped with a cane or beaten with a strap—also did not work.

Parents of children with a learning disability often search desperately for a program to help their children. It can be difficult for parents to be at the mercy of schools and teachers who are victims of bureaucracy and not allowed to use helpful techniques. Sometimes schools are unresponsive, or the problem is so severe that it requires intensive intervention. Many problems at school can be eliminated if we search for the underlying cause of school difficulties at a young age and intervene when the child is in the early grades.

For parents of children with learning disabilities, there are some useful web-based discussion groups, including LDExperience (www.ldexperience.ca) and LD OnLine (www.ldonline.org). They provide important information and the opportunity to pose questions and join in the discussions. Another resource with practical advice for parents is the Helpguide page on learning disabilities (www.helpguide.org/topics/learning-disabilities.htm). Support groups for parents, whether in the community or online, can help both them and their children to navigate the challenges of a child with a learning disability.

27

The Road Ahead

Learning disabilities represent a very serious problem for society. They can have profound effects on children and youth. Having a learning disability increases the chance that a young person will end up homeless and living on the street, and possibly engaging in prostitution, substance abuse, and/or criminal activities. Of course, this is not the fate of most people with learning disabilities, but it is a tragedy that happens too often.

The stories of Agatha Christie, Susan Hampshire, Greg Louganis, William Butler Yeats, Pablo Picasso, Hans Christian Andersen, and Winston Churchill when they were children are typical of cases found in today's clinics for children with learning disabilities. Their stories have happy endings but, unfortunately, the lives of many children with learning disabilities do not. People with undetected and untreated learning disabilities can end up in jail, living on the streets of big cities, committing suicide as adolescents, and/or abusing alcohol and illicit drugs.

Most of these outcomes could have been avoided with early detection and treatment of learning disabilities.

Street Youth

The correct identification of learning disabilities is critical for the health of individuals and our society. If we fail to identify and help these individuals, the results can be disastrous. According to research that Melanie Barwick and I conducted, 83 per cent of the homeless youth ("street kids") we tested in Toronto, Canada, have learning disabilities that have not been properly recognized or treated.[1] We conducted this study at a drop-in centre for homeless youth, and with their consent, we tested their reading, spelling, and mathematics skills. These young people really wanted help for their learning problems, but they were too old for the educational system to help them. Their learning disabilities are not the result of a difficult home life or substance abuse or a disadvantaged economic background. The 17 per cent of the street youth in this study who did not have learning disabilities came from identical backgrounds as the youth who did. One of the reasons that these young people ended up homeless and on the street was that their learning disabilities were not addressed by the schools. Undetected and untreated learning disabilities are a significant factor in anti-social behaviour. Many young people in the correctional system or in custody, and other individuals in prison, have learning disabilities that have not been identified or treated.[2] As you saw in chapter 21, Jason, a young man who committed suicide, also ended up on the street because the school system ignored his learning problems and destroyed his self-esteem.

Solutions

Solving the problem of learning disabilities can be straight-forward and inexpensive. We need proper identification of learning disabilities and excellent strategies to help people when we find problems. If we put what we know into practice, we would save millions of dollars and many lives.

One of the most important solutions to the problem of learning disabilities is the early identification of children at risk for learning problems. There are two aspects to identification. One is the early identification of children at risk for potential problems before they have experienced the humiliation of failure and at a time when it is easiest for them to learn. The other aspect is the detection of actual learning problems in older children and adults. Our school systems are failing on both accounts.

We know how to discover potential reading problems when a child is five years old. A simple, inexpensive, and reliable screening test of vocabulary, language, and phonological aware-ness skills is all that is needed to detect children at risk for reading problems. The purpose of this screening is not to label or blame, but to help teachers understand the child's strengths and weaknesses.[3]

Ideally, this screening should be done with even younger children, but at this time we do not have a reliable way of doing so. We also do not yet have reliable ways of detecting children *at risk* for mathematics, spelling, and/or writing difficulties, but hope-fully future research will bring the necessary tools. We should put our efforts, financial and otherwise, into the early identification of children at risk for these problems.

Testing for Learning Disabilities

As I have discussed in earlier chapters, we need to have a much simpler and more reliable way of identifying learning disabilities in elementary, secondary, and post-secondary students and adults. Currently the process is very complex, expensive, and time-consuming, taking up to three to five hours to test one person. Not all these tests are necessary.

As I wrote in chapter 11, to assess whether or not there are learning problems, tests of reading words and pseudowords, reading comprehension, spelling, mathematics, and writing should be administered routinely to all students. For the reasons discussed earlier, IQ tests are not necessary. If students have low scores on an achievement test, they should get remedial help without worrying about whether they are *really* learning disabled. All children and adults should have access to clinics where they can be tested to determine whether or not they have a learning disability.

Once we identify the problems, we need to provide the best remedial instruction and accommodations that we can. Educators should help develop students' strengths as well as address their weaknesses. Artistic, musical, athletic, and other talents should be fostered and celebrated.

Early Intervention

Once the identification of a learning disability has been made, it is important to follow it with some sort of intervention. It is much easier to treat children when they are young than to wait for the problems to get more serious and until children are the victims of teasing and bullying from classmates or peers. It costs ten times as much to treat an older child with reading problems as to treat a younger one.[4]

The North Vancouver school district in British Columbia, Canada, has developed a program called Firm Foundations that helps develop skills related to early reading.[5] It concentrates on developing early language skills and teaches vocabulary, rhyming, breaking words into syllables and phonemes (the smallest units of sound in a word), and recognizing initial sounds. The program consists of interactive games and activities that teach the children basic skills in a fun manner. We have found that this program is effective with children whose first language is English and with children who have English as a second language but are being educated in English. The children play games and engage in activities to help develop their language skills. This program reduced the incidence of dyslexia from 25 per cent at the start of the program to about 2 per cent.

Response to Intervention (RTI)

There are some promising innovations in programming that can really help children with learning disabilities. One of these new techniques is Response to Intervention (RTI). RTI is based on the idea that it is important to provide intervention early, before the child experiences failure. The emphasis in RTI is not on diagnosis; instead it is on intervention. RTI happens in three tiers. In the first tier, there is good classroom instruction. If children are struggling, then they should get help immediately, without waiting for a diagnosis. If intervention in the first tier fails, then they move to the second tier, where the instruction becomes more intensive, usually in small groups. If they are still struggling in the second tier, they move to the third tier, in which they receive intensive intervention on a one-to-one basis and/or in a specialized classroom. Of course, this type of RTI is an innovative idea that is often not the reality in school systems. But it is a worthy goal to aim for.

Universal Design for Learning (UDL)

Another educational intervention is Universal Design for Learning (UDL), which is based on the premise that instruction should be designed for individuals and should consider their strengths and weaknesses.[6] There are three basic principles. The first is "multiple means of representation," which means that information can be conveyed in many ways. For example, some people learn better from hearing a lecture about a topic and others learn better when they read the material. Some prefer pictures and diagrams; others have difficulty interpreting them. The second principle is "multiple means of expression." There are a variety of ways to demonstrate your knowledge: by writing, speaking, drawing, acting out a play, and so on. The third tenet is called "multiple means of engagement"; it means that learners have different motivations, interests, and backgrounds that should be considered in educating them. UDL helps us understand the individual learner and ideally should help provide a variety of educational alternatives.

The Peter Effect, or Why Teacher Education Matters

Good teacher education is essential to improving schooling for all children. Almost twenty years ago, Louisa Moats, an expert on dyslexia and teaching how to read conducted studies of teachers of reading or students who were preparing to teach reading and found that the majority did not know some of the important basics of the English language.[7] For example, they did not know the number of sounds in a word (*king* has three sounds) or that *th* is one sound, called a consonant blend. She sounded the alarm but her warnings went unheeded.

Recently, Dr. Maltesta Joshi, an international expert on learning difficulties, found similar results. He reviewed textbooks used in teacher education programs and concluded that they do not provide adequate information about dyslexia or how to teach children with reading problems.[8] He also found misinformation in textbooks. For example, some books still describe dyslexia as a visual deficit, ignoring the years of research showing that it is a language deficit. He conducted surveys of students in teacher education programs and found results similar to those Louisa Moats found; namely, that teachers of language do not understand some of the basic aspects of English phonics. He used the term the "Peter Effect" with regard to teacher education, which states: you cannot be expected to give what you do not possess.[9] Joshi concluded that teacher education programs are not adequately teaching students about reading difficulties or preparing them to teach reading. Unless this situation changes, we will not see much progress in helping children with reading difficulties.

Fiddling While Rome Burns, or Ignoring the Problems

Governments, departments of education, ministries of education, and school districts in all parts of the world fail to adequately address the problem of students with learning disabilities. Sometimes, they suggest very superficial "solutions." Here are some helpful suggestions for providing solutions:[10]

- Teach the basic skills involved in reading, mathematics, and writing to all students in school. Sometimes this instruction happens; sometimes it does not. It is shocking that teacher education programs do not always teach about learning disabilities and how to effectively teach mathematics, reading, and writing. The lack of direct and systematic instruction in teaching mathematics and reading skills is simply appalling and is a result of the failure of teacher education. An unknown number of children (and adults) are catastrophes of the educational system. Recent educational innovations such as Response to Intervention and Universal Design for Learning can provide good models for helping all children.

- Use screening techniques to identify children at risk early in their school career and provide intervention as soon as there are any signs of difficulty.

- Provide services for all students who are struggling, without resorting to extensive testing and a diagnosis. The waiting time for testing can be as long as two years, which is frustrating for the child, the teacher, and the parents. Teach the teachers how to do brief testing to identify any learning difficulties that a child may have, give them the tools to do the testing, and trust their judgement and commitment to the job.

- Eliminate the time-wasting and useless filling out of forms and meetings. In many school systems, for a child to get special education help, the teacher and school staff must fill out forms that are sometimes as long as twenty pages. Sometimes the system requires meetings to be held among teachers, parents, and other professionals before the system makes a diagnosis and decides to help a child. These meetings are time-consuming, difficult to arrange, and inefficient. Of course, initial meetings with parents and teachers and school administrators are important to clarify the needs of the child and to address any difficulties, but requiring many professionals to be involved is counterproductive. While waiting for the forms to be filled out and read, or the meeting to occur, the child suffers.

• School systems need to respect parents and listen to what they say. In my many years of dealing with parents and school systems, I have encountered few parents who are unreasonable or unrealistic about their children. These few parents can pose a challenging problem for the school system, but most parents start out being respectful of teachers and school personnel and listening to what they say. Unfortunately, parents are sometimes treated badly, and they may then become resentful and hostile, and the situation escalates. However, most adversarial situations could be avoided if school administrators and teachers listened respectfully to parents.

Final Thoughts

There will always be people who struggle with reading, writing, spelling, and mathematics, just as there will always be people like me who cannot carry a tune. This should not stop us from trying to help people with learning disabilities as much as possible. It is not an excuse for failing to identify the learning problem early, providing good teaching, and trying to understand the strengths of people with learning disabilities. Agatha Christie, William Butler Yeats, Winston Churchill, and many others were able to succeed despite learning problems, but they did so with help, with supportive families, and because they were given the chance to develop their abilities. So let school systems and families search hard for each person's talents and make sure that each individual has the opportunity to develop his or her talents, in spite of learning difficulties.

The message is clear. Find the problems early and do not assume that children who have difficulty with reading, spelling, or arithmetic are merely being difficult. Teach them using a variety of strategies—visual, kinesthetic, and verbal. Celebrate their talents. Never call them stupid or lazy or emotionally disturbed. Educators who failed to understand and provide help for their learning problems have ruined too many children's lives. Parents and teachers must learn to recognize the signs of learning disabilities. If a child is having problems learning to read or spell or print or do mathematics, then these difficulties are signs of possible learning disabilities.

Sometimes behavioural problems, such as aggression towards other children or defying authority or appearing to be unconcerned with doing homework, are signs of a learning disability. Behavioural problems often get misinterpreted. One young man related that for a long time his school referred to him as having "an attitude problem" rather than dealing with his learning disability. He ran into difficulties with peers and school staff. He got into numerous fights at school. He would often bring his anger and frustration home from school as well. Once he threw his lunchbox against the wall after a particularly difficult day.

Learning difficulties cause problems with self-esteem, which can lead children to act out to get the attention or approval of their peers. Sometimes children with learning problems can be easily led to do inappropriate actions to get approval. One girl whom I tested confessed that her "friends" urged her to shoplift some candy. When she was a bit older, she recognized how vulnerable she had been.

Parents should be alert for signs of school phobia. If a child has stomach aches on Mondays or weekdays but these pains disappear on the weekend, this may be a sign of a learning disability. Remember, however, that sometimes a stomach ache is just a stomach ache. One Monday morning my six-year-old daughter told me that she had a stomach ache. She had shown no signs of a learning disability, but I was alert to possible behavioural signs. I asked her if she felt well enough to go to school and she said yes. Shortly after she entered the classroom, I received a call from the school telling me that she had vomited. I learned my lesson. The flu is not a sign of school phobia.

If children become withdrawn or have tantrums, these are possible signs of a learning disability. Be alert to bullying and teasing. Children may be ashamed to talk about it and feel that it is their fault.

What is the difference between individuals with learning disabilities who end up on the street or as criminals or committing suicide, and those who lead productive lives? Most often, the difference is having sensitive, helpful, non-critical parents, and schools and teachers who help them develop their strengths and make accommodations to help them learn and help build their self-esteem and sense of self worth. Self-esteem is fragile in all of us, and especially in people with learning disabilities, who often experience failure, scorn, and merciless teasing. Self-esteem must be fostered and developed, not destroyed.

Many of society's serious problems, including anti-social behaviour, homelessness, and suicide, can be reduced if we identify learning disabilities and provide appropriate help to people who have them. Lives are wasted, even ruined, by not developing the skills and talents of people with learning disabilities. Solving the puzzle of learning disabilities will not cure all the evils in the world, but it would be a giant step forward.

Acknowledgements

I would like to thank all the children, adults, and parents who have so graciously participated in my research projects.

I thank Catherine Edwards, Nadine Pedersen, and Barbara Kuhne of Pacific Educational Press for believing in this project and using their skills and experience to make it a reality. I thank Barbara Kuhne for her superb editing. She assisted greatly in developing the structure and flow of the book. I thank Sharlene Eugenio for the design and layout, Kaye Banez and Natalia Cornwall for their marketing skills, and Grace Yaginuma for copy editing the manuscript.

My colleague and friend Keith Stanovich contributed immeasurably to my understanding of reading, reasoning, data analysis, and dyslexia.

Gina Harrison contributed very useful and constructive comments on earlier drafts of this book.

Jane Rosenman and Martha Morrison made many helpful comments on earlier drafts.

Fran Blackwood and Shar Levine provided encouragement and graciously shared their stories with me.

A special thank-you to Zanna Downes for all her help.

I owe a tremendous debt of gratitude to the real Johnny for so graciously sharing his story; the real Darryl for generously sharing his experiences and report cards with me; the real Paul and his parents and the real Rob and his parents for sharing their stories; and the real Jason's mother for sharing her story. The trauma she experienced should never have been allowed to happen. My heart goes out to her in her suffering, which could have been avoided by a more vigilant, co-operative, and sensitive school district.

A big thank-you to Greg Louganis for graciously granting permission for me to use excerpts from his book, *Breaking the Surface*.

I thank Isabel Shessel for sharing her work with me. I am proud to have had her as a student.

I thank Kathryn Burke and Colin Reid for sharing their stories.

I am grateful to the David and Dorothy Lam Foundation for supporting my Dorothy C. Lam Chair in Special Education in the Faculty of Education at the University of British Columbia.

Many of the ideas in this book were developed during my term as a Scholar in Residence at the Peter Wall Institute for Advanced Studies at UBC. I thank the Institute for this wonderful opportunity.

The following people shaped my thinking and helped me understand the complexities of learning disabilities: Phil Abrami, Salim Abu Rabia, Marilyn Adams, Katie Adelstein, Daniel Ansari, Terry Au, Hadas Av Gay, Liz Barrett, Melanie Barwick, Christian Beaulieu, Lorna Bennett, Elaine Benton, Andy

Biemiller, Judith Boel, Chuck Brainerd, Liz Bredberg, Zvia Breznitz, Monique Brodeur, Stan Brosman, Maggie Bruck, Eva Bures, Catharine Byers, Norlan Cabot, Claudia Cardoso-Martins, Anna Cassar, Lisa Cesario, Carol Chan, Eva Chan, Victoria Chaney, Kevin Cheung, Chi Yanping, Penny Collins, Morna Collis, Debbie Cooper, Cesare Cornoldi, Carolyn Cowen, Judy Craig, Chuck Cunningham, Karin Dahlin, Karin Dakin, Kathryn D'Angelo, Amedeo D'Angiulli, Hans Dekkers, Molly DeLemos, Suzanne Dery, Susan de Stein, Adele Diamond, Silvia DiFior, Stuart Farson, Philippe Fellerath, Jack Fletcher, Laurie Ford, David Francis, Nicole Fusaro, Isabel Galli de Pampliega, Kathryn Garforth, Esther Geva, Debbie Giaschi, Luigi Girolametto, Laurie Goegan, Vincent Goetry, Alex Gottardo, Elena Grigorkeno, Lee Gunderson, Judit Gyenes, Carol Hall, Katie Hall, Sylvia Hannah, Ruth Hayhoe, Kerry Hempenstall, Kari Hewitt, Norm Himel, Erland Hjelmquist, Connie Ho, F. C. Ho, Barbara Hodkin, Fumiko Hoeft, Juan Jimenez, Catherine Johnson, Heather Kaney, Lynne Kent, Ellen Knell, Maggie Koong, Michelle Kozey, Gail Krivel Zacks, Karen Kwok, Alice Lai, Glen Lawson, Suk Han Lee, Thealzel Lee, Marie Therese LeNormand, Christiana Leonard, Nonie Lesaux, the late Margaret Lesperance, Pearl Levey, Jenn Liang, Bruce Linder, Orly Lipka, John Lloyd, Morgaine Longpre, Pauline Low, Daniela Lucangeli, the late Ingvar Lundberg, William Ma, Alex MacKay, Stefania Maggi, Stefka Marinova-Todd, Silvia Mazabel, Michele Mazzocco, Cammie McBride, Hazel McBride, Mary McBride, Peggy McCardle, Lynne McGivern, Maureen McQuarrie, Jamie Metsala, John Mighton, Lynn Miller, Marylou Miner, Louisa Moats, Tori and Dennis Molfese, Tina and Frank Moore, Fred Morrison, Kristen Morrison, the late Sylvia Morrison, Jo-Anne Naslund, Roslyn

Neilson, Dena Ocampo, Randi O'Connor, Anaberta Oehler, Arlene and Peter Ommundsen, Pam Ottley, Mary Padden, Julia Pan, Marita Partanen, Chiara Passolunghi, Rufina Pearson, Pei Miao, Michele Pentyliuk, Chuck Perfetti, Neil Pinkerton, Filiz Polat, Franky Poon, Wes Pue, Qiang Haiyan, Raffi, Nirmala Rao, Catherine Remedios, Urs Ribary, Michaele Robertson, Diane Rose, Susie Russak, Judith and Stewart Sanson, Rob Savage, Hollis Scarborough, Anat Scher, Tyson Schoeber, Emily Serra, Uri Shafrir, David Share, Penny Shepherd-Hill, Phillipa Slater, Ian Smythe, Johnny Solity, Rick Sparks, Liliane Sprenger-Charolles, Nancy Stein, Karla Stuebing, Laura Super, Rosemary Tannock, Tom Tjus, Suk Man Tsang, Sharon Vaughn, Ludo Verhoeven, Rose Vukovic, Lesly Wade-Woolley, Barry Wansbrough, Brendan Weekes, Janet Werker, Barbro Westlund, Kevin and Robyn Wheldall, Jim and Joan White, Judy Wiener, Dale Willows, Ulrika Wolff, Bernice Wong, Richard Wong, Craig Wright, Susanna Yeung, Zhao Lin, Zhao Wei, Zhou Jing, and Bruno Zumbo.

Thanks to Susan, Stephen, and the late Peter Hart for sharing their insights.

Thanks to my children, Laura and Jeffrey, for their support and giving me such wonderful grandchildren. I also thank Lois and Toby for their encouragement.

My special thanks go to David for his support, patience, enthusiasm, and encouragement.

— Linda Siegel, Salt Spring Island, Canada

Notes

Chapter 1: The Giant with Dyslexia

1. This chapter draws on the seven Harry Potter books by J. K. Rowling: *Philosopher's Stone, Chamber of Secrets, Prisoner of Azkaban, Goblet of Fire, Order of the Phoenix, Half-Blood Prince,* and *Deathly Hallows*.
2. The movie *Harry Potter and the Sorceror's Stone* was the first movie in the series, released in 2001.
3. Rowling, *Order of the Phoenix*, 395–97.

Chapter 2: Spelling Test Terror

1. This account is based on a true story. I have changed the boy's name and some details to protect his identity.
2. See, for example: Siegel, in "Phonological Processing Deficits and Reading Disabilities." Also see: Siegel, in "Cognitive Basis of Dyslexia" and in "Phonological Processing Deficits as the Basis."
3. Shaywitz, Shaywitz, Fletcher, and Escobar, "Prevalence of Reading Disability."
4. Siegel and Smythe, "Reflections on Research."
5. Shaywitz, Fletcher, et al., "Persistence of Dyslexia."
6. West, *In the Mind's Eye*.
7. Details of the life of Albert Einstein are from a biography. See Isaacson, *Einstein: His Life and Universe*.

Chapter 3: Picasso, the Artist with Dyslexia

1. Sabartés, *Picasso: An Intimate Portrait.*
2. Picasso, *Picasso, My Grandfather*, 19.
3. Richardson, *A Life of Picasso*, 42.

Chapter 4: The Case of Agatha Christie: Dysgraphia

Parts of this chapter were adapted from Siegel, "Agatha Christie's Learning Disability."
The chapter epigraph is from Christie, *An Autobiography*, 47.

1. Ibid., 26.
2. Morgan, *Agatha Christie: A Biography*, 20.
3. Christie, *An Autobiography*, 118.
4. Feinman, *Mysterious World of Agatha Christie*, 20–21.
5. Murdoch, *The Agatha Christie Mystery*, 41.
6. Woodcock, McGrew, and Mather, *Woodcock-Johnson III Tests of Achievement.*
7. Ibid.

Chapter 5: Winston Churchill—Famous Orator, Superb Military Strategist, Failure at Mathematics

The chapter epigraph is from Churchill, *My Early Life*, 34.

1. Ibid., 47.
2. Ibid., 34.
3. Ibid., 33.
4. See, for example: Siegel, in "Reproductive, Perinatal, and Environmental Factors."
5. Churchill, *My Early Life*, 38.
6. This account is based on a true story. I have changed the boy's name and some details to protect his identity.

Chapter 6: Hans Christian Andersen: A Case of Non-Verbal Learning Disability

1. The information in this chapter comes from Hans Christian Andersen's autobiography, *The Fairy Tale of My Life*, and from the following biographies: Bredsdorff, *Story of His Life and Work*; Godden, *Great Life in Brief*; Stirling, *Wild Swan*; and Toksvig, *Life of Hans Christian Andersen.*
2. Toksvig, *Life of Hans Christian Andersen*, 93.

3. Andersen, *Fairy Tale*, 45.
4. Toksvig, *Life of Hans Christian Andersen*, 84
5. Stirling, *Wild Swan*, 92.
6. Toksvig, *Life of Hans Christian Andersen*, 92.
7. Stirling, *Wild Swan*, 93.
8. Godden, *Great Life in Brief*, 96.
9. Galway and Metsala, "Social Cognition and Its Relation to Psychosocial Adjustment."
10. Bredsdorff, *Story of His Life and Work*, 215.

Chapter 7: Yeats, the Poet with Dyslexia

Parts of this chapter were adapted from Miner and Siegel, "William Butler Yeats: Dyslexic?"

The chapter epigraph is from Yeats, *Autobiographies*, 5–6.

1. Ibid., 23.
2. Jeffares, *W. B. Yeats: A New Biography*, 9.
3. Ibid., 32.
4. Yeats, *Autobiographies*, 24.
5. Foster, *W. B. Yeats: A Life*, 17.
6. Yeats, *Autobiographies*, 47.
7. Ibid., 56
8. Ibid., 41.
9. Ibid., 56.
10. Ibid., 58.
11. Ibid., 57.
12. Ibid., 57.
13. Ibid., 56.
14. Ibid., 5–6.
15. Ibid., 102–3.

Chapter 8: Jane Austen: The First Educational Psychologist

1. Austen, *Northanger Abbey*, 37.
2. Ibid., 39.
3. Ibid., 38.
4. Ibid., 37–38.
5. Ibid., 40.
6. Ibid., 38.

7. Ibid., 38.

8. Ibid., 40.

9. Ibid., 37.

Chapter 9: "Stupid Tom": George Eliot on Dyslexia

The chapter epigraph is from Eliot, *Mill on the Floss*, 127.

1. Ibid., 14.

2. Ibid., 147.

3. Ibid., 51.

4. Ibid., 152.

5. Ibid., 124.

6. Ibid., 125.

7. Ibid., 124.

8. Gardner, *Frames of Mind.*

9. Eliot, *Mill on the Floss*, 7–8.

10. Ibid., 8.

11. Ibid., 14.

Chapter 10: The Scientific Discovery of Dyslexia

1. Pringle Morgan, "A Case of Congenital Word Blindness."

2. Ibid.

3. Hinshelwood, "A Case of Congenital Word-Blindness."

4. Orton, " 'Word-Blindness' in School Children."

5. Ibid., 582.

6. Ibid., 587.

7. Miller and Westman, "Reading Disability as a Condition of Family Stability."

8. Danforth, *Incomplete Child*, 190–91.

Chapter 11: Tiptoeing through the Minefield of Diagnosis

1. Some of the ideas in this chapter were previously expressed in Siegel's "Confessions and Reflections of the Black Sheep."

2. See, for example: Siegel, in "Issues in the Definition and Diagnosis." Also see: Siegel and Metsala, in "Alternative to the Food Processor Approach"; Siegel and Heaven, in "Categorizing Learning Disabilities"; and Siegel, Levey, and Ferris, in "Subtypes of Developmental Dyslexia."

3. See, for example: Lennox and Siegel, in "Development of Phonological Rules." Also see: Lennox and Siegel, in "Visual and

Phonological Spelling Errors" and in "Phonological and Orthographic Processes."

Chapter 12: IQ Worship: Into the Quicksand

1. Some of the ideas in this chapter were previously expressed in Siegel's "Confessions and Reflections of the Black Sheep."
2. Gardner, *Frames of Mind*.
3. Dove, "The 'Chitling' Test."
4. See, for example: Siegel, in "IQ Is Irrelevant." Also see: Siegel, in "Evidence That IQ Scores Are Irrelevant"; and Stanovich and Siegel, in "Phenotypic Performance Profile."
5. Kozey and Siegel, "Definitions of Learning Disabilities."
6. Siegel, "Evaluation of the Discrepancy Definition." A number of other studies have found the same results. See, for example: Fletcher, Shaywitz, et al., in "Cognitive Profiles of Reading Disability"; Fletcher, Francis, et al., in "Validity of Discrepancy-Based Definitions"; and Stuebing, Barth, et al., in "IQ Is Not Strongly Related."
7. Siegel and Smythe, "Importance of Phonological Processing."
8. See, for example: Tal and Siegel, "Pseudoword Reading Errors." Also see: Stuebing, Fletcher, et al., "Validity of IQ-Discrepancy Classification."
9. Siegel, "Evidence That IQ Scores Are Irrelevant."
10. Stuebing, Barth, et al., "IQ Is Not Strongly Related."
11. Tanaka et al., "Brain Basis of the Phonological Deficit in Dyslexia."
12. Kozey and Siegel, "Definitions of Learning Disabilities."

Chapter 13: Abuses of the IQ Test: The Case of Johnny

1. Excerpts from Johnny's story are from personal correspondence with the author.

Chapter 14: Not Stupid: A Tale of Two Teachers

1. Pennac, *School Blues*, 53.

Chapter 15: Not Lazy: The Case of Darryl

1. This account is based on a true story. I have changed the man's name and some details to protect his identity.

Chapter 16: Reading Is a Goose Flying: Learning Disabilities through the Eyes of Children

1. This chapter draws on a research project headed by Dr. L. Jin of De

Montfort University, UK, in collaboration with the Dyslexia Association of Singapore. All quotations are from Jin et al., "Perceptions and Strategies of Learning in English."

Chapter 17: The Albatross, or Living with a Learning Disability

1. The material in this chapter draws on my interviews with children and adults with learning disabilities, the parents of children with learning disabilities, and the following books: Edwards, *Scars of Dyslexia*; Guyer, *Pretenders*; Riddick, *Living with Dyslexia*; and Riddick, Farmer, and Sterling, *Students and Dyslexia*. I also refer to a doctoral thesis: Shessel, "Adults with Learning Disabilities: Profiles in Survival."
2. McBride and Siegel, "Learning Disabilities and Adolescent Suicide."
3. Burke, "What Makes a Good Teacher (for a Kid with Learning Disabilities)?," *Kathryn's Column* (blog), LDExperience, May 1, 2012, www.ldexperience.ca/what-makes-a-good-teacher-for-a-kid-with-learning-disabilities-by-kathryn-burke/.

Chapter 18: Becoming Rhinoceros-Skinned: Learning to Jump the Hurdles

1. Shessel, "Adults with Learning Disabilities: Profiles in Survival." Also see: Shessel, in "Adults with Learning Disabilities: Overcoming the Odds"; and Shessel and Reiff, in "Experiences of Adults with Learning Disabilities."
2. Shessel, "Adults with Learning Disabilities: Profiles in Survival," 156.
3. Ibid., 191.
4. Ibid., 149.
5. Ibid., 150.
6. Ibid., 112.
7. Ibid., 153.
8. Ibid., 154.
9. Ibid., 155.
10. Ibid., 158.
11. Ibid., 158.
12. Ibid., 160.
13. Ibid., 161.
14. Ibid., 161.
15. Ibid., 165.
16. Ibid., 165–66.
17. Ibid., 166.

18. Ibid., 181.

19. Ibid., 133.

20. Ibid., 181.

21. Ibid., 132.

22. Ibid., 153.

Chapter 20: Dyslexia and Murder?

1. Rendell, *A Judgement in Stone*, 7.

2. Ibid., 37.

3. Ibid., 57.

4. Ibid., 127–28.

5. Ibid., 136.

6. Ibid., 136–37.

7. Ibid., 141.

8. Ibid., 55.

9. Ibid., 159.

10. Ibid., 7.

11. Ibid., 48.

12. Ibid., 48.

13. Ibid., 55.

14. Ibid., 7.

15. Ibid., 41.

16. See, for example: Johnson et al., in "Television Viewing and Aggressive Behavior." Also see: Huesmann et al. in "Longitudinal Relations between Children's Exposure."

17. Rendell, letter to author, June 13, 1994.

18. Rendell, interview.

Chapter 21: A Parent's Worst Nightmare

1. This account is based on a true story. I have changed the names of those involved and some details to protect their identities.

2. Personal interview with Ms. Edwards. Other information in this account is based on several interviews with her.

Chapter 23: Drowning, Diving, and Surfacing

The chapter epigraph is from Louganis, *Breaking the Surface*, 39.

1. Ibid., 35.

2. Ibid., 39.

3. Ibid., 36.
4. Olweus, *Bullying at School.*
5. Louganis, *Breaking the Surface*, 90.
6. Ibid., 27.
7. Ibid., 27.
8. Ibid., 18.
9. Ibid., 113.
10. Ibid., 264.
11. Ibid., xii.

Chapter 24: Teaching Basic Skills

1. See, for example: Hall and Moats, *Straight Talk about Reading.* Also see: Hall and Moats, in *Parenting a Struggling Reader*; and Polacco, in *Thank You*, Mr. Falker and in *The Art of Miss Chew.*
2. Riordan, *The Lightning Thief, The Sea of Monsters, The Titan's Curse*, and *The Battle of the Labyrinth.*
3. Perry, *Rose of No Man's Land, Tudor Rose, Blood Red Rose*, and *Rose between Two Thorns.*
4. See "Dyslexia-Friendly Books" at www.lovereading4kids.co.uk /genre/dys/Dyslexia-friendly.html, accessed April 2, 2013.
5. Mighton, *Myth of Ability* and *End of Ignorance.*

Chapter 25: Technology and Other Ways of Helping People with Learning Disabilities

1. Yau, Siegel, and Ziegler, "Laptop Computers and the Learning Disabled Student."
2. Fink, "Literacy Development in Successful Men and Women."

Chapter 26: The Great Cover-Up: What Parents Should Know to Avoid Being Victims of the System

The chapter epigraph is from D. Reist, February 26, 2012, participant in the thread "LD Identified as a Behavior Problem," LD OnLine Discussion Boards, www.ldonline.org/xarbb/ (forums accessible by members only).

1. Ibid.
2. R. Slabich, March 2, 2012, participant in "LD Identified as a Behavior Problem."
3. S. Blumberg, March 4, 2012, participant in "LD Identified as a Behavior Problem."
4. P. McGuire, March 13, 2012, participant in "LD Identified as a Behavior Problem."

5. Davis, Moldaver LLP Barristers letter to author, December 5, 2008.

6. Siegel, "The Arrowsmith Program."

7. "Your Questions Answered" (FAQ), accessed April 2, 2013, www.dore.co.uk/programme/faq/.

8. Stephenson and Wheldall, "Miracles Take a Little Longer."

Chapter 27: The Road Ahead

1. Barwick and Siegel, "Learning Difficulties in Adolescent Clients."

2. See, for example: Foley, in "Academic Characteristics of Incarcerated Youth." Also see: Katsiyannis et al., in "Juvenile Delinquency and Recidivism"; and Rogers-Adkinson et al., in "Language Competency of Incarcerated Youth."

3. See, for example: Lesaux and Siegel, in "Development of Reading." Also see: Siegel, in "Reducing Reading Difficulties"; Lipka and Siegel, in "Early Identification and Intervention"; and Siegel, in "Remediation of Reading Difficulties."

4. Nicolson et al., "Early Reading Intervention Can Be Effective."

5. See the Firm Foundations website at www.nvsd44.bc.ca/Firm foundations/main.html. The North Vancouver School District has also developed a program called Reading 44 (www.nvsd44.bc.ca/Reading44/main.html) that is very useful for reading and writing instruction. To learn about resources available to teachers and how to order them, click on "Firm Foundations" or "Reading 44" under "Educational Resources" on the North Vancouver School District website (www.nvsd44.bc.ca).

6. Hall, Meyer, and Rose, *Universal Design for Learning in the Classroom*.

7. Moats, "The Missing Foundation," *American Federation of Teachers*; and "The Missing Foundation," *Annals of Dyslexia*.

8. Joshi et al., "Textbooks Used in University"; and Washburn, Joshi, and Cantrell, "Are Preservice Teachers Prepared?"

9. Applegate and Applegate, "The Peter Effect."

10. Freedman, a Boston attorney, expressed some of these ideas in "4 Common-Sense Proposals." Although we agree on many of these issues, I stress early identification and intervention, focused but not extensive psychoeducational testing, and a more collaborative approach among parents, teachers, and school administrators.

Bibliography

Andersen, H. C. *The Fairy Tale of My Life: An Autobiography.* Translated from the Danish. 1871. Reprint, New York: Paddington Press, 1975.

Applegate, A. J., and M. D. Applegate. "The Peter Effect: Reading Habits and Attitudes of Teacher Candidates." *The Reading Teacher* 57 (2004): 554–63.

Austen, J. *Northanger Abbey.* 1818. Penguin Classics edition. London: Penguin Books, 1985. Page references are to the 1985 edition.

Barwick, M. A., and L. S. Siegel. "Learning Difficulties in Adolescent Clients of a Shelter for Runaway and Homeless Street Youths." *Journal of Research on Adolescence* 6 (1996): 649–70.

Bredsdorff, E. *Hans Christian Andersen: The Story of His Life and Work 1805–75.* London: Phaidon, 1975.

Burke, K. *An Accidental Advocate: A Mother's Journey with Her Exceptional Son.* Edmonton, AB: Sextant, 2011. Also available as an e-book from Smashwords.

Burke, K. "What Makes a Good Teacher (for a Kid with Learning Disabilities)?" *Kathryn's Column* (blog), LDExperience, May 1, 2012. www.ldexperience.ca/what-makes-a-good-teacher-for-a-kid-with-learning-disabilities-by-kathryn-burke/.

Christie, A. *An Autobiography.* London: Collins, 1977.

Churchill, W. S. *My Early Life: 1874–1908*. Glasgow: Collins, 1979. W.S. first published 1930.

Corcoran, J. *The Teacher Who Couldn't Read*. New York: Kaplan, 1994.

Danforth, S. *The Incomplete Child: An Intellectual History of Learning Disabilities*. New York: Peter Lang, 2009.

Dove, A. "The 'Chitling' Test." In *Psychological and Educational Testings*, Lewis R. Aiken, Jr. Boston: Allyn and Bacon, 1971. Accessed online at wilderdom.com/personality/intelligenceChitlingTestShort.html.

Edwards, J. *The Scars of Dyslexia*. London: Cassell, 1994.

Eliot, G. *The Mill on the Floss*. 1860. London: Everyman, 1996. Page references are to the 1996 edition.

Feinman, J. *The Mysterious World of Agatha Christie*. New York: Award Books, 1975.

Fink, R. "Literacy Development in Successful Men and Women with Dyslexia." *Annals of Dyslexia* 48 (1998): 311–46.

Fletcher, J. M., D. J. Francis, B. P. Rourke, S. E. Shaywitz, and B. A. Shaywitz. "The Validity of Discrepancy-Based Definitions of Reading Disability." *Journal of Learning Disabilities* 25 (1992): 555–61.

Fletcher, J. M., S. E. Shaywitz, D. P. Shankweiler, L. Katz, I. Y. Liberman, K. K. Stuebing, and B. A. Shaywitz. "Cognitive Profiles of Reading Disability: Comparisons of Discrepancy and Low Achievement Definitions." *Journal of Educational Psychology* 86 (1994): 6–23.

Foley, R. M. "Academic Characteristics of Incarcerated Youth and Correctional Educational Programs: A Literature Review." *Journal of Emotional and Behavioral Disorders* 9, no. 4 (2001): 248–59.

Foster, R. F. *W. B. Yeats: A Life*. Vol. 2, *The Apprentice Mage: 1865–1914*. New York: Oxford University Press, 1998.

Freedman, M. K. "4 Common-Sense Proposals for Special Education Reform." *The Atlantic*, April 27, 2012. Accessed online at www.theatlantic.com/national/archive/2012/04/4-common-sense-proposals-for-special-education-reform/256435/.

Galway, J. M., and J. L. Metsala. "Social Cognition and Its Relation to Psychosocial Adjustment in Children with Nonverbal Learning Disabilities." *Journal of Learning Disabilities* 44 (2011): 33–49.

Gardner, H. *Frames of Mind: The Theory of Multiple Intelligences*. 10th anniversary ed. New York: Basic Books, 2004.

Godden, R. *Hans Christian Andersen: A Great Life in Brief*. New York: Alfred A. Knopf, 1955.

Guyer, B. *The Pretenders: Gifted People Who Have Difficulty Learning.* Homewood, IL: High Tide Press, 1997.

Hall, S. L., and L. C. Moats. *Parenting a Struggling Reader.* New York: Broadway Books, 2002.

————. *Straight Talk about Reading: How Parents Can Make a Difference During the Early Years.* Lincolnwood, IL: Contemporary Books, 1999.

Hall, T. E., A. Meyer, and D. Rose, eds. *Universal Design for Learning in the Classroom: Practical Applications.* New York: Guilford Press, 2012.

Hampshire, S. *Susan's Story.* London: Sphere Books, 1983.

Harry Potter and the Sorceror's Stone. Directed by Chris Columbus. 2001. Burbank, CA: Warner Brothers, 2002. DVD.

Hinshelwood, J. "A Case of Congenital Word-Blindness." *The Ophthamoscope* 22 (1904): 399–405.

Huesmann, L. R., J. Moise-Titus, C. Podolski, and L. D. Eron. "Longitudinal Relations between Children's Exposure to TV Violence and Their Aggressive and Violent Behavior in Young Adulthood: 1977–1992." *Developmental Psychology* 39 (2003): 201–21.

Isaacson, W. *Einstein: His Life and Universe.* New York: Simon and Schuster, 2007.

Jeffares, A. N. *W. B. Yeats: A New Biography.* New York: Farrar, Straus and Giroux, 1988.

Jin, L., K. Smith, A. Yahya, A. Chan, M. Choong, V. Lee, V. Ng, P. Poh-Wong, and D. Young. "Perceptions and Strategies of Learning in English by Singapore Primary School Children with Dyslexia—A Metaphor Analysis." *British Council ELT Research Papers*, no. 11-03 (2011): 1–23. Available online at www.teachingenglish.org.uk/publications/perceptions-strategies-learning-english-singapore-primary-school-children-dyslexia.

Johnson, J. G., P. Cohen, E. M. Smailes, S. Kasen, and J. S. Brook. "Television Viewing and Aggressive Behavior during Adolescence and Adulthood." *Science* 295 (2002): 2468–71.

Joshi, R. M., E. Binks, L. Graham, E. Ocker-Dean, D. L. Smith, and R. Boulware-Godden. "Do Textbooks Used in University Reading Education Courses Conform to the Instructional Recommendations of the National Reading Panel?" *Journal of Learning Disabilities* 42 (2009): 458–63.

Katsiyannis, A., J. Ryan, D. Zhang, and A. Spann. "Juvenile Delinquency and Recidivism: The Impact of Academic

Achievement." *Reading and Writing Quarterly* 24 (2008): 177–96. doi:10.1080/10573560701808460.

Kozey, M., and L. S. Siegel. "Definitions of Learning Disabilities in Canadian Provinces and Territories." *Canadian Psychology* 49 (2008): 162–71.

Lennox, C., and L. S. Siegel. "The Development of Phonological Rules and Visual Strategies in Average and Poor Spellers." *Journal of Experimental Child Psychology* 62 (1996): 60–83.

———. "Phonological and Orthographic Processes in Good and Poor Spellers." In *Reading and Spelling: Development and Disorders*, edited by M. Joshi and C. Hulme, 395–404. New Jersey: Erlbaum, 1998.

———. "Visual and Phonological Spelling Errors in Subtypes of Children with Learning Disabilities." *Applied Psycholinguistics* 14 (1993): 473–88.

Lesaux, N. K., and L. S. Siegel. "The Development of Reading in Children Who Speak English as a Second Language." *Developmental Psychology* 25 (2003): 1005–19.

Lipka, O., and L. S. Siegel. "Early Identification and Intervention to Prevent Reading Difficulties." In *Literacy Development and Enhancement across Orthographies and Cultures*, edited by D. Aram and O. Korat, 205–19. Literacy Studies, vol. 2. New York: Springer, 2010.

Louganis, G. *Breaking the Surface*. With E. Marcus. NY: Random House, 1995.

Mann, T. *Confessions of Felix Krull, Confidence Man: The Early Years*. New York: Alfred A. Knopf, 1955. Reprint. New York: Vintage International, 1992.

Mazzocco, M. A., and G. F. Myers. "Complexities in Identifying and Defining Mathematics Learning Disability in the Primary School-Age Years." *Annals of Dyslexia* 53 (2003): 218–53.

McBride, H., and L. S. Siegel. "Learning Disabilities and Adolescent Suicide." *Journal of Learning Disabilities* 30 (1997): 652–59.

Mighton, J. *The End of Ignorance: Multiplying Our Human Potential*. Toronto: Alfred Knopf, 2007.

———. *The Myth of Ability: Nurturing Mathematical Ability in Every Child*. Toronto: House of Anansi Press, 2003.

Miller, D. R., and J. C. Westman. "Reading Disability as a Condition of Family Stability." *Family Process* 3 (1964): 66–76.

Miner, M., and L. Siegel. "William Butler Yeats: Dyslexic?" *Journal of Learning Disabilities* 25 (1992): 372–75.

Moats, L. C. "The Missing Foundation in Teacher Education." *American Federation of Teachers* 9 (Summer 1995): 45–51.

———. "The Missing Foundation in Teacher Education: Knowledge of the Structure of Spoken and Written Language." *Annals of Dyslexia* 44 (1994): 81–102.

Morgan, J. *Agatha Christie: A Biography.* London: Collins, 1984.

Murdoch, D. *The Agatha Christie Mystery.* Toronto: Wiley, 1976.

Nicolson, R. I., A. J. Fawcett, H. Moss, M. K. Nicolson, and R. Reason. "Early Reading Intervention Can Be Effective and Cost-Effective." *British Journal of Educational Psychology* 69 (1999): 47–62.

Niven, L., and J. Pournelle. *Inferno.* New York: Pocket Books, 1976.

Olweus, D. *Bullying at School: What We Know and What We Can Do.* Oxford: Wiley-Blackwell, 1993.

Orton, S. T. "'Word-Blindness' in School Children." *Archives of Neurology and Psychiatry* 5 (1925): 581–615.

Pennac, D. *School Blues.* Translated by Sarah Ardizzone. London: MacLehose Press, 2010.

Perry, A. *Blood Red Rose.* Edinburgh, UK: Barrington Stoke, 2012

———. *Rose between Two Thorns.* Edinburgh, UK: Barrington Stoke, 2012.

———. *Rose of No Man's Land.* Edinburgh, UK: Barrington Stoke, 2011.

———. *Tudor Rose.* Edinburgh, UK: Barrington Stoke, 2011.

Picasso, M. *Picasso, My Grandfather.* In collaboration with L. Valentin. Translated by Catherine Temerson. New York: Riverhead Books, 2001.

Polacco, P. *The Art of Miss Chew.* New York: Putnam, 2012.

———. *Thank You, Mr. Falker.* New York: Philomel Books, 1998.

Pringle Morgan, W. "A Case of Congenital Word Blindness." *The British Medical Journal* 1871 (1896): 1378.

Rendell, R. Interview by J. W. Ross. In vol. 32 of *Contemporary Authors*, edited by J. G. Lesniak, 362–64. Detroit: Gale Research, 1991.

Rendell, R. *A Judgement in Stone.* London: Hutchinson, 1977.

Richardson, J. *A Life of Picasso.* Vol. 1, *1881–1906.* New York: Random House, 1991.

Riddick, B. *Living with Dyslexia.* London: Routledge, 1996.

Riddick, B., M. Farmer, and C. Sterling. *Students and Dyslexia: Growing Up with a Specific Learning Disability.* London: Whurr, 1997.

Riordan, R. *The Battle of the Labyrinth.* New York: Scholastic, 2009.

————. *The Lightning Thief.* New York: Scholastic, 2005.

————. *The Sea of Monsters.* New York: Scholastic, 2007.

————. *The Titan's Curse.* New York: Scholastic, 2008.

Rogers-Adkinson, D., K. Melloy, S. Stuart, L. Fletcher, and C. Rinaldi. "Reading and Written Language Competency of Incarcerated Youth." *Reading and Writing Quarterly* 24, no. 2 (2008): 197–218.

Rowling, J. K. *Harry Potter and the Chamber of Secrets.* Vancouver: Raincoast Books, 1999.

————. *Harry Potter and the Deathly Hallows.* New York: Arthur A. Levine Books, 2007.

————. *Harry Potter and the Goblet of Fire.* Vancouver: Raincoast Books, 2000.

————. *Harry Potter and the Half-Blood Prince.* Vancouver: Raincoast Books, 2005.

————. *Harry Potter and the Order of the Phoenix.* Vancouver: Raincoast Books, 2003.

————. *Harry Potter and the Philosopher's Stone.* Vancouver: Raincoast Books, 1997.

————. *Harry Potter and the Prisoner of Azkaban.* Vancouver: Raincoast Books, 1999.

Sabartés, Jaime. *Picasso: An Intimate Portrait.* Translated by Angel Flores. London: W.H. Allen, 1948.

Shaywitz, S. E., J. M. Fletcher, J. M. Holahan, A. E. Shneider, K. E. Marchione, K. K. Stuebing, D. J. Francis, K. R. Pugh, and B. A. Shaywitz. "Persistence of Dyslexia: The Connecticut Longitudinal Study at Adolescence." *Pediatrics* 104 (1999): 1351–59. Cited in M. M. Mazzocco and G. F. Myers, "Complexities in Identifying and Defining Mathematics Learning Disability in the Primary School-Age Years," in *Annals of Dyslexia* 53 (2003): 218–53.

Shaywitz, S. E., B. A. Shaywitz, J. M. Fletcher, and M. D. Escobar. "Prevalence of Reading Disability in Boys and Girls: Results of the Connecticut Longitudinal Study." *Journal of the American Medical Association* 264 (1990): 998–1002.

Shessel, I. "Adults with Learning Disabilities: Overcoming the Odds." *Abilities Magazine,* Spring 1997.

————. "Adults with Learning Disabilities: Profiles in Survival." EdD thesis, University of Toronto, 1995.

Shessel, I., and H. B. Reiff. "Experiences of Adults with Learning Disabilities: Positive and Negative Impacts and Outcomes." *Learning Disability Quarterly* 22 (1999): 305–16.

Siegel, L. S. "Agatha Christie's Learning Disability." *Canadian Psychology* 29 (1988): 213–16.

————. "The Arrowsmith Program: The Triumph of Hype over Science." *LDA (Learning Difficulties Australia) Bulletin* 44 (2012): 29–31.

————. "The Cognitive Basis of Dyslexia." In *Competencies*, 33–52. Vol. 2 of *Emerging Themes in Cognitive Development*, edited by R. Pasnak and M. L. Howe. New York: Springer-Verlag, 1993.

————. "Confessions and Reflections of the Black Sheep of the Learning Disabilities Field." *Learning Difficulties Australia* 17 (2012): 63–77.

————. "An Evaluation of the Discrepancy Definition of Dyslexia." *Journal of Learning Disabilities* 25 (1992): 618–29.

————. "Evidence That IQ Scores Are Irrelevant to the Definition and Analysis of Reading Disability." *Canadian Journal of Psychology* 42 (1988): 201–15.

————. "IQ Is Irrelevant to the Definition of Learning Disabilities." *Journal of Learning Disabilities* 22 (1989): 469–78, 486.

————. "Issues in the Definition and Diagnosis of Learning Disabilities: A Perspective on Guckenberger v. Boston University." *Journal of Learning Disabilities* 32 (1999): 304–19.

————. "Phonological Processing Deficits and Reading Disabilities." In *Word Recognition in Beginning Literacy*, edited by L. Ehri and J. Metsala, 141–60. Mahwah, NJ: Erlbaum, 1998.

————. "Phonological Processing Deficits as the Basis of Developmental Dyslexia: Implications for Remediation." In *Cognitive Neuropsychology and Cognitive Rehabilitation*, edited by M. J. Riddoch and G. W. Humphreys, 379–400. Hove, UK: Erlbaum, 1994.

————. "Reducing Reading Difficulties in English L1 and L2: Early Identification and Intervention." In *Dyslexia Across Languages: Orthography and the Brain-Gene-Behavior Link*, edited by P. McCardle, B. Miller, J. R. Lee, and O. J. L. Tzeng, 294–304. Baltimore, MD: Paul H. Brookes, 2011.

————. "Remediation of Reading Difficulties in English Language

Learning Students." In *How Children Learn to Read*, edited by K. Pugh and P. McCardle, 275–88. New York: Psychology Press, 2009.

———. "Reproductive, Perinatal, and Environmental Factors as Predictors of the Cognitive and Language Development of Preterm and Full-Term Infants." *Child Development* 53 (1982): 963–73.

Siegel, L. S., and R. Heaven. "Categorizing Learning Disabilities." In *Handbook of Cognitive, Social, and Neuropsychological Aspects of Learning Disabilities*, edited by S. Ceci, 1:95–121. Hillsdale, NJ: Erlbaum, 1986.

Siegel, L. S., P. Levey, and H. Ferris. "Subtypes of Developmental Dyslexia: Do They Exist?" In *Applied Developmental Psychology*, edited by F. J. Morrison, C. Lord, and D. P. Keating, 2:169–90. New York: Academic Press, 1985.

Siegel, L. S., and J. Metsala. "An Alternative to the Food Processor Approach to Subtypes of Learning Disabilities." In *Learning Disabilities: Nature, Theory, and Treatment*, edited by N. N. Singh and I. L. Beale, 44–60. New York: Springer-Verlag, 1992.

Siegel, L. S., and I. S. Smythe. "The Importance of Phonological Processing Rather Than IQ Discrepancy in Understanding Adults with Reading Disorders." In *Adult Learning Disorders: Contemporary Issues*, edited by L.E. Wolf, H.E. Schreiber, and J. Wasserstein, 275–300. New York: Psychology Press, 2008.

———. "Reflections on Research on Reading Disability with Special Attention to Gender Issues." *Journal of Learning Disabilities* 5 (2005): 473–77.

Stanovich, K. E., and L. S. Siegel. "The Phenotypic Performance Profile of Reading-Disabled Children: A Regression-Based Test of the Phonological-Core Variable-Difference Model." *Journal of Educational Psychology* 86 (1994): 24–53.

Stephenson, J., and K. Wheldall. "Miracles Take a Little Longer: Science, Commercialisation, Cures and the Dore Program." *Australasian Journal of Special Education* 32, no. 1 (2008): 67–82.

Stirling, M. *The Wild Swan: The Life and Times of Hans Christian Andersen*. New York: Harcourt, Brace and World, 1965.

Stuebing, K. K., A. E. Barth, P. J. Molfese, B. Weiss, and J. M. Fletcher. "IQ Is Not Strongly Related to Response to Reading Instruction: A Meta-analytic Interpretation." *Exceptional Children* 76 (2009): 31–51.

Stuebing, K. K., J. M. Fletcher, J. M. LeDoux, G. R. Lyon, S. E. Shaywitz, and B. A. Shaywitz. "Validity of IQ-Discrepancy Classification of Reading Disabilities: A Meta-analysis." *American Educational Research Journal* 39 (2002): 469–518.

Tal, N. F., and L. S. Siegel. "Pseudoword Reading Errors of Poor, Dyslexic and Normally Achieving Readers on Multisyllable Pseudowords." *Applied Psycholinguistics* 17 (1996): 215–32.

Tanaka, H., J. M. Black, C. Hulme, L. M. Stanley, S. R. Kesler, S. Whitfield-Gabrieli, A. L. Reiss, J. D. E. Gabrieli, and F. Hoeft. "The Brain Basis of the Phonological Deficit in Dyslexia Is Independent of IQ." *Psychological Science* 22, no. 11 (2011): 1442–51.

Toksvig, S. *The Life of Hans Christian Andersen*. London: MacMillan, 1934.

Washburn, E. K., R. M. Joshi, and E. B. Cantrell. "Are Preservice Teachers Prepared to Teach Struggling Readers?" *Annals of Dyslexia* 61, no. 1 (2011): 21–43.

West, T. G. *In the Mind's Eye*. Buffalo, NY: Prometheus, 1991.

Woodcock, R. W., K. S. McGrew, and N. Mather. *Woodcock-Johnson III Tests of Achievement*. Itasca, IL: Riverside, 2001.

Yau, M., L. S. Siegel, and S. Ziegler. "Laptop Computers and the Learning Disabled Student." *ERS Spectrum* 9 (1991): 22–30.

Yeats, W. B. *Autobiographies*. London: Macmillan, 1956.

Permissions

The author and publisher gratefully acknowledge the permission granted to reproduce the copyright material in this book. Every effort has been made to trace copyright holders and to obtain their permission for the use of copyright material. The publisher apologizes for any errors or omissions in the list below and would be grateful if notified of any corrections that should be incorporated in future printings or editions of this book.

Chapter 4
This chapter is adapted from an earlier version of Linda Siegel's "Agatha Christie's Learning Disability," *Canadian Psychology* 29 (1988): 213–16. Used by permission of the Canadian Psychological Association.

Chapter 16
Quotations from Lixian Jin et al.'s "Perceptions and Strategies of Learning in English by Singapore Primary School Children with Dyslexia—A Metaphor Analysis," *British Council ELT Research Papers*, no. 11-03 (2011): 1–23, are used by permission.

Chapter 17
Quotations from Colin Reid, from Kathryn Burke's "What Makes a Good Teacher (for a Kid with Learning Disabilities)?," *Kathryn's Column* (blog),

LDExperience, May 1, 2012 (www.ldexperience.ca/what-makes-a-good-teacher-for-a-kid-with-learning-disabilities-by-kathryn-burke/), are used by permission of Kathryn Burke.

Chapter 18

Quotations from Isabel Shessel's "Adults with Learning Disabilities: Profiles in Survival," EdD thesis, University of Toronto, 1995, are used by permission.

Chapter 19

Quotations from Ruth Rendell's *A Judgement in Stone*, London: Hutchinson, 1977, are reprinted by permission of the Random House Group Limited.

Chapter 23

Quotations from Greg Louganis's *Breaking the Surface*, with Eric Marcus, New York: Random House, 1995, are used by permission of Greg Louganis.

Chapter 26

Quotations from Don Reist, Rena Slabich, Susan Blumberg, and Patricia McGuire, participants in the thread "LD Identified as a Behavior Problem" on the LD OnLine Discussion Boards (www.ldonline.org/xarbb/), are used by their permission.

Index

Linda Siegel is a professor in the Department of Educational and Counselling Psychology and Special Education at the University of British Columbia, Vancouver, Canada, where she holds the Dorothy C. Lam Chair in Special Education. She has conducted research on the development of reading and of mathematical concepts, language development, dyslexia, mathematical learning disabilities, early identification and intervention to prevent reading difficulties, and the development of reading and language skills in children learning English as a second language. She has consulted on the development of reading skills in elementary school age children in China (Hong Kong, Xian, Guangzhou, and Shen Zhen), Barbados, Brazil, Argentina, Switzerland, and many places in the US and Canada. In 2010, she was awarded the Gold Medal for Distinguished Contributions to Canadian Psychology from the Canadian Psychological Association. In 2012, she received the inaugural Eminent Researcher Award from the organization Learning Difficulties Australia. She has been awarded an honorary doctorate from the University of Gothenburg (Sweden).